*To Margaret, who brings an even keel
to my books and to life*

Table of Contents

Preface

ᨎ᷈⟶

About every 18 months, I have released a new book on technology-enabled innovation. Then last December, I detoured and wrote *SAP Nation*, an exposé on waste in information technology (IT). One of the findings in the book: "So, in effect, for $2 billion in annual development budget outlays, SAP customers are paying over $200 billion a year to its ecosystem."

When that book was published, I was all set to resume writing about digital transformations. And yet, after just eight months, I find myself writing more about the SAP economy. You might wonder, "why?"

Firstly, SAP announced its next-gen S/4HANA (S/4) product in February 2015. As a result, several readers and consulting clients wanted feedback on what that meant for their strategies. Secondly, seemingly out of the woodwork, in reaction to the many customers profiled in *SAP Nation*, I started hearing from/ about other SAP users. The common thread was, "I wish you had talked to us when you wrote the book—here is what we [or so-and-so customer] are doing to optimize our SAP environment."

Thirdly, I got abundant feedback about the book's model of the SAP economy—many thought that I had under-estimated the already scary, annual $200 billion in customer spending.

Analyzing the likely S/4 impact and hearing about the plethora of customer strategies has made me increasingly aware of the diversity in SAP environments. SAP's own product portfolio has exploded, with nearly 50 acquisitions in the last decade. Additionally, there is organic growth in its own product lines. SAP customer environments are even more diverse, with a wide range of satellite apps (most non-SAP) and customizations. Further, the SAP ecosystem is rapidly expanding with the addition of Fiori consultants, HANA start-ups and private cloud providers.

SAP's marketing is all about "simple" and every partner is amplifying that "simple" message. Well, is it truly simple? This sequel to *SAP Nation* keeps asking that question.

When you layer in SAP's product portfolio on top of its customers' application portfolios and the 13,000 partners it claims, a different six-letter word that also starts with 'S' comes to mind: Sprawl.

SAP's runaway success in the '90s came about because its R/3 product dramatically reduced enterprise sprawl. Can history repeat itself? Will S/4 replace today's sprawl, this time caused by SAP itself?

The book is structured as following:

> Chapter 1 takes an in-depth look at SAP's product portfolio, applications implemented at its customers and the diversity in its partner ecosystem.

Chapter 2 looks at the rolling launch of S/4, details of which have been dribbling out over the past several months.

Chapter 3 explores many of the questions that keep coming up about S/4 that SAP will need to address.

Chapter 4 delves into two decades of enterprise software vendor attempts at next-gen products. We look at projects at Infor, JD Edwards, Microsoft, Oracle and SAP itself. How will S/4 reflect the sum of all these previous industry experiences?

Chapter 5 assesses the economic impact the rollout of S/4 may have on the $200+ billion annual gross domestic product (GDP) of the SAP economy. It also takes into account further feedback I have received on the SAP economy model.

Chapter 6 describes the wide range of SAP customer coping strategies I have been hearing about in the last few months.

Finally, Chapter 7 provides guidance for SAP to consider as it continues to roll out S/4. The chapter also catalogs ideas to help customers insulate themselves in an economy with no Central Bank and no real oversight—an Empire in Disarray.

Some readers will ask, "Should I read *SAP Nation* before reading this sequel?" While not critical, it would definitely help, and I encourage readers to focus on the 30+ case studies in that book. Additionally, readers will appreciate history from the 1990s and 2000s with many of SAP's acquisitions and pivots, and even more a steady stream of spectacular SAP customer project failures.

Others may ask, "When can we expect 'SAP Nation 3.0'?" I intend to work in the role of an advisor with SAP customers as the S/4 transition unfolds, and hopefully, this will give me enough material to write the next installment.

In the meantime, I would like to revert to writing about digital transformations, observing what SAP customers are doing to make their own products, services and business models more digital, even as they wait for SAP and its partners to make their back offices slimmer and more agile.

July 2015

CHAPTER 1

The End of History?

∿→

In 1989, as the Cold War was ending, Francis Fukuyama, a political scientist, asked whether it was, "The End of History?"[1] His optimistic essay, which projected that the world was getting ready to adopt what he called "capitalist liberal democracy," appeared in a relatively small publication, *The National Interest*. It still garnered an amazing amount of interest and Fukuyama has since written several books and influenced foreign policy.

So much has changed since 1989, as I was reminded as I listened to a keynote earlier in 2015 by former U.S. Secretary of State, Dr. Condoleezza Rice, now back in academia. As she spoke, my mind drifted to several trips I have made to Eastern Europe. It was a sobering talk about geopolitics, with several humorous moments, especially when she described how Russian

---

[1] https://ps321.community.uaf.edu/files/2012/10/Fukuyama-End-of-history-article.pdf

President Vladimir Putin would always flatter her about her knowledge as a "Sovietologist."

Yes, we used to have specialists whose job it was to understand the complex sprawl behind the Iron Curtain. It was a vast empire spread across 11 time zones and covered a wide range of cultures and languages. I have often wondered how Moscow kept such an empire intact for so long.

The diversity and distances reminded me that SAP Nation (my term for that company's vast ecosystem) is like the Eastern Bloc of the 1980s. SAP's product portfolio has exploded, and in the last decade there have been nearly 50, seemingly disconnected acquisitions. That has led Mark Hurd, CEO of competitor Oracle (itself very acquisitive), to sarcastically observe, "I guess we could buy a Dairy Queen."

Then there is their own organic product growth, where SAP has released over 50 country-specific SAP Business All-in-One baseline solutions in the latest SAP-HANA-enabled enhancement package. SAP Business One, with over 50,000 smaller customers around the world, is not exactly dead. Even its Business ByDesign (BYD), which has suffered from a series of SAP missteps, has been called "alive and kicking."[2]

SAP says over 7,000 customers are using HANA, which means the majority of its nearly 300,000 customers are still persisting with databases from Oracle, Microsoft, IBM and SAP's own Sybase and MaxDB. In periodic updates, SAP shows the state of support for Oracle's Database version 10g, 11g, 12c, its

---

[2] http://diginomica.com/2014/10/23/sap-business-bydesign-alive-kicking/#at_pco=tst-1.0&at_si=54f973438669d968&at_ab=per-2&at_pos=0&at_tot=2

engineered systems and related products.[3] That diversity will continue for years, as customers will not jettison the elaborate systems management and talent infrastructures they have built around those databases.

Liz Herbert, an analyst at Forrester, wrote about the diversity around the HANA product alone:

> "Clients struggle to keep up with the rapidly evolving landscape of Hana—an ever-growing list of solutions that includes Hana, Hana cloud, Hana Enterprise Cloud, S/4 Hana, Simple Finance, and others."[4]

Customers comment they see an SAP with "multiple personalities." When they meet Dr. Hasso Plattner, it is the "HANA SAP." When they meet CEO Bill McDermott, it is the "business networks SAP" (reflecting the Ariba, Concur and Fieldglass side of the business). Then they meet vertical executives and they are assured their industry is the most important.

When Oracle launched its acquisition spree a decade ago, SAP had marketed itself as a "Safe Harbor" to customers of the acquired companies. That has changed dramatically with a customer observing, "SAP used to have a not-invented-here mindset. Now, it is a 'net-new' mindset. They are constantly trying to get new revenues from us."

---

[3] http://www.sdn.sap.com/irj/scn/go/portal/prtroot/docs/library/uuid/e01c4e88-9f5a-2d10-a5b3-e53cb577baee?QuickLink=index&overridelayout=true&60168196896845

[4] https://www.forrester.com/SAP+Hana+Promises+To+Revolutionize+CX+But+Clients+Struggle+To+Find+The+Right+Partner/fulltext/-/E-res122903

This opportunistic talk was on display in a *Fortune*[5] magazine interview of McDermott. He mostly talked about the "new SAP"—HANA, Ariba, Concur, SuccessFactors, hybris, Fieldglass, Sybase—while taking for granted customers will continue to send in maintenance checks for the old SAP:

> "SAP will remain ever strong in the core. There are many customers that run very sophisticated global businesses on that core. They've invested heavily in it. . . . That core is rock-solid. I call it Fort Knox."

At SAPPHIRE NOW, in May 2015, SAP Digital announced a new set of products including a CRM solution at $29 per user per month. SAP claims to now have 17 million Jam users and 2,000 HANA start-ups. The executives responsible for such SAP initiatives proudly brag about them, even though they contribute merely 1–2 percent of SAP revenues, and they keep adding to the sprawl.

SAP's runaway success in the '90s came about because its R/3 product dramatically reduced enterprise sprawl. As Paul Melchiorre, one of its most successful salespeople had noted in *SAP Nation:* "It was a truly transformational time for the technology industry. We replaced thousands of departmental and mainframe systems. We put MSA, M&D, and many others out of business. We didn't really have much competition. In deals it would be SAP v. SAP v. SAP—that is, SAP/Accenture v. SAP/KPMG v. SAP/PwC."

---

[5] http://fortune.com/2015/01/27/qa-bill-mcdermott-ceo-sap/

Today, SAP's cloud competitors are using that very argument against it. Dave Duffield, co-founder of Workday likes to describe having customers on a common code base as the "power of one". Zach Nelson, CEO of NetSuite touts "one product for many industries".

Next, there is the sprawl around SAP's core applications at its customers.

I cannot help but think of the massive landmass and diversity of cultures that was the former U.S.S.R. when you look at all the satellite apps run by SAP customers and their millions of lines of customization code. According to Panaya, a tool vendor, "More than 50% of SAP shops have 40+ satellite applications. Of these less than 10 are SAP applications." CAST Research Labs has analyzed customizations at several major SAP customers and found most of the customizations were sizable, with many of them high-risk, according to its benchmarks.

Finally, there is significant growth in the partner ecosystem. At its Global Partner Summit this year, SAP announced it now has 13,000 partners—a five-fold increase in the last decade.[6] There are many newer and smaller Fiori- and HANA-focused consultants, plus all the HANA start-ups mentioned above and many new private cloud hosting providers. SAP application management is morphing as those providers automate and move to as-a-service business models. The SAP-acquired companies like SuccessFactors and existing products like Business One are seeing churn in their implementation/reseller channels.

---

[6] http://blogs.gartner.com/robert-anderson/2015/06/04/sap-global-partner-summit-ushers-in-partneredge-2-0/

The continuing challenge is that SAP likes to use the large counts of users, customers and partners for marketing advantage, but does not invest enough in infrastructure to manage that scale. When I questioned why VC firms tend to invest only in a handful of start-ups they can appropriately fund and manage, while SAP was seeking thousands of HANA startups, an executive from SAP rationalized:

> "Being startups, a large percentage of these firms will stumble along the way and only a small fraction of the ones remaining will achieve breakout success. It is hard to know in advance which ones these will be but I am very keen to find out. This is one reason we've spread the net far and wide. As SAP, we can only try to approach this with humility and do our best to do our part in this endeavor."[7]

The wide diversity in SAP's portfolio and its customer base is vividly on display in its advertising budget. This runs the gamut, from radio spots promoting the Concur product to small businesses, SuccessFactors billboards at competitor events, corporate branding at hockey stadiums, three-page spreads in *The Wall Street Journal*, hot air balloons and HANA commercials which ask "Can a business have a mind, a spirit, a soul?" It would appear every taxi driver, sports fan and New Age practitioner who can influence software decisions is being targeted. This marketing carries over to social media, where SAP executives

---

[7]   https://www.enterpriseirregulars.com/71991/sap-hana-ecosystem-excitement-caution/

and fans rave about individual products as if they represent the whole SAP economy.

A Nation of Underdogs?

On this side of the pond, in a patriotic July 4 (U.S. Independence Day) guest column titled, "A nation of underdogs," McDermott wrote:

> "From equal rights activists to entrepreneurs, our nation's history is rife with stories of people who believed the impossible was possible. Indeed, a notion that an underdog can win—whatever his definition of winning may be—is part of our country's DNA. It's a truism I know firsthand."[8]

He then shared his life story with that preface. Most executives fiercely protect their private lives. McDermott has been unusually transparent about his personal life, as *Business Insider* notes:

> "He was born to a working class family in Long Island, full of love, setbacks, and heartbreak. McDermott has poured out his whole amazing life story in a new book, "Winners Dream." The book is part memoir and part business strategy."[9]

---

[8] http://www.foxnews.com/opinion/2015/07/03/nation-underdogs.html?intcmp=sbox2_pam

[9] http://www.businessinsider.com/saps-bill-mcdermott-rags-to-riches-2014-11#ixzz3fIpA7QjY

Some say this candor indicates that McDermott is getting ready to enter politics. Others say that this is the real McDermott, a positive, inspirational leader who is driven to take SAP to greater heights. In my dealings with him, I have always admired his demeanor—he is polite and attentive, and I doubt he even knows we share birthdays.

McDermott would benefit from spending some time with urban planners regardless of his career plans. As part of the book research about sprawl, I reached out to an old college mate, Dr. Russell Fricano, who has had a career in community planning, zoning administration and environmental review. Dr. Fricano was a regional planner for Los Angeles County and now teaches Urban Planning. He shared with me some research on the impact of urban sprawl.

From one paper:

> "Sprawl has engendered six major crises for America's major metropolitan regions. These crises are: (1) central city and first- and second-ring suburban decline; (2) environmental degradation through loss of wetlands, sensitive lands and air and water quality degradation; (3) massive gasoline energy overutilization; (4) fiscal insolvency, infrastructure deficiencies, and taxpayer revolts; (5) devastating agricultural land conversion; and (6) housing inaffordability."[10]

---

[10] The Social Costs of Sprawl, Robert H. Freilich and Bruce G. Peshoff, The Urban Lawyer. Vol. 29. No. 2 (Spring 1997).

From another:

> "Sprawl produces a 21% increase in amount of unde-
> veloped land converted to developed land (2.4 million
> acres) and approximately a 10% increase in local road
> lane-miles (188300). Furthermore, sprawl causes about
> 10% more annual public service (fiscal) deficits ($4.2 bil-
> lion) and 8% higher housing occupancy costs ($13000
> per dwelling unit)."[11]

These papers might as well be talking about the waste and inefficiency in SAP Nation. SAP shops lag IT industry benchmarks in many categories—cost per function point, speed of upgrades and cost of IT infrastructure per user. The project failures in the SAP economy have been spectacular and show little sign of slowing down.

An SAP alum told me he was impressed at how McDermott has grown during his decade at the company. "He came from a copier background. I did not think he would adapt to the complex world of enterprise software."

In that decade, however, enterprise tech itself has evolved dramatically with social, mobile, analytical and cloud computing. Substantial local recruiting has not helped SAP's image in Silicon Valley, where Amazon, Box, Cloudera, Docker, Salesforce, and even Oracle are increasingly considered the "cool" enterprise vendors.

---

[11] Conventional Development versus Managed Growth: The Costs of Sprawl, Robert W. Burchell, PhD, and Sahan Mukherji. BS, American Journal of Public Health, September 2003, Vol 93, No 9

McDermott could inspire the "underdogs" in SAP Nation to tackle the sprawl challenge. With his sales background, he has proven his ability to generate new revenue. The SAP economy, however, does not need more selling. The economy needs "unselling"—delivering on previous promises, lowering prices to reflect new market realities, and more predictable results. If McDermott can pull that off, it could be his lasting legacy at SAP. Dr. Plattner has certainly raised expectations with his own "end of history" statement. After introducing the next-gen product, S/4HANA in early 2015, he told a journalist, "If this doesn't work, we're dead. Flat-out dead."[12]

Will SAP Nation have a smooth transition with its recently announced S/4 or will it be chaotic, with people sighing in relief as they exit its airspace? Will it fragment into many parts as the Soviet Union did if its shareholders decide the parts are better spun off from the whole? Will we continue to need "SAPologists" to understand what is happening in that complex economy? Will SAP and its partners continue to long for the bloated past and will the economy balloon even more than its already inflated annual $200 billion run rate? Will McDermott's "underdogs" deliver a stunning turnaround?

The end of history? Before we jump too far ahead, let's look at the launch of S/4 in February 2015.

---

[12] http://www.businessinsider.com/sap-founder-hasso-plattner-if-this-doesnt-work-were-dead-2015-2

CHAPTER 2

One More Thing

∿⟶

"If ecosystem is confused how must customers feel?" asked a tweet from Greg Misiorek, a consultant.

In a conversation, Marc Kustoff, CIO of Endo International, a global pharma company, provided an answer to that very question:

> "I have been a big champion of SAP at my current and previous companies because I believe that when properly applied, an integrated SAP environment can be a unifying, transformational platform that can dramatically improve a company's effectiveness and profitability. SAP has been trying to articulate that it understands the transition to the cloud, but it has not connected all the dots yet. So I expect their messaging will be a bit muddled until they develop a crisper vision of how to get there within their technical and functional environment."

An executive at another global SAP customer also used the word "muddled" in a similar conversation:

> "I am a reasonably smart person, and I am struggling. SAP's thinking these days appears as muddled as it was when it introduced mySAP in 2000 and it attempted to show it understood the then-emerging Web economy."

At another large SAP customer, an executive was even more blunt:

> "I doubt I will see this in my shop before I retire in the 2020s . . . the amount of work to get to HANA is staggering, and I have not seen a coherent road map yet."

Karenann Terrel, CIO of Walmart joked on stage at SAPPHIRE NOW:

> "I hope to see S4/HANA delivered in my lifetime. It's on my bucket list."[13]

We are used to seeing crowds line up for blocks when Apple introduces a new product. In comparison, the SAP launch of S/4 would qualify as a non-event, with media reports still using words like "demystifying" and "lingering questions" months after its launch.

The Art of the Product Launch

Who does not like new and shiny? Professors at Harvard and Michigan have noticed a trend:

---

[13] http://blog.vdcresearch.com/mobile_and_wireless/2015/05/event-recap-sap-sapphire-mobile-perspective.html

"Consumers act more recklessly with their current products and are less concerned about losing or damaging them when in the presence of appealing product upgrades."[14]

As an innovation author, I find one of the most enjoyable topics to write about is the birth of new products and initiatives. Product launches have become increasingly sophisticated. You have to marvel at how Apple managed the launch of the 3G version of the iPhone in 2008. It was launched in 22 countries, followed by 50 more countries over the next few months. The logistics of producing tens of millions of units with its contract manufacturer, Foxconn in China, then shipping them around the world via FedEx and coordinating with hundreds of country-specific phone companies has raised the bar for complex yet well-coordinated product launches.

I have also written about new versions of humbler products like Lexmark printers, more complex products like Boeing planes and breakthrough data centers like those at Facebook. I like to talk to the designers, marketers and project managers about how they decided on which features to include, the engineering challenges they faced, the launch logistics and the risks they balanced.

So, when McDermott announced a next-generation product in February 2015, "our biggest launch in 23 years, if not in the entire history of the company," I was excited and went back and re-read some of the case studies in my books and the questions I had asked of each:

- Would SAP acknowledge that the ERP market was languishing like Lexmark did when launching the Genesis

---

[14] http://papers.ssrn.com/sol3/papers.cfm?abstract_id=2590322

printer in 2010: "How do you get consumers excited about a significant form/factor leap in a device with a boring and frustrating image?"[15]

- Would SAP rethink its supply chain like Boeing did when it created the Dreamlifter for its new 787 program? The Dreamlifter is a modified 747 used to transport major portions of the new plane from suppliers in Italy, Japan and many other countries to the final assembly site in Everett, Washington. This allowed Boeing to reduce shipping times to as little as one day from as much as 30 days that it would normally take via sea and ground transport.

- Would SAP dramatically reduce waste like Facebook did when it told its suppliers to ship "vanity-free" servers to its data center in Prineville, Oregon? The servers were delivered with no plastic bezels, paint or even mounting screws—saving Facebook significant dollars in manufacturing, packaging and assembly costs.

- Would there be econometric planning for SAP Nation to help retrain a couple of million "citizens" and rethink its aging data center and network infrastructure? Would it, like Singapore's Workforce Development Agency, prepare its citizens with an Individual Learning Portfolio that allows them to transition into newer skills and careers, so the workforce on that island state stays relevant from one decade to the next?

---

[15] http://www.amazon.com/New-Technology-Elite-Consumption-Production/dp/1118103130/ref=sr_1_1?ie=UTF8&qid=1435868012&sr=8-1&keywords=the+new+technology+elite

Another Forced March?

Balancing my excitement, I had to factor in the caution that customers have shown about upgrades in their on-premise enterprise software, and especially in SAP World. Nir Paikowsky, Senior Director of Product Management & Product Marketing, SAP product line at Panaya (now part of Infosys), encapsulated it well for me:

> "With modern software, and especially with mobile devices, we have become accustomed to seeing quick adoption cycles of new software releases and version updates. The Google Android adoption trend graph in Exhibit 1 is a classic example of this.
>
> However, for on-premise Enterprise Software, such adoption cycles are significantly longer, and in many cases getting such visibility is nearly impossible, even for the software vendor itself.

Google Android – Version Adoption Trend

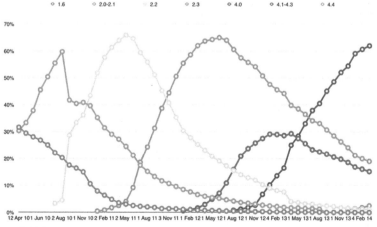

Exhibit 1　　　　　　　　　　Source: Jackdaw Research

At Panaya, as an SaaS tool vendor focusing on assisting customers with changes to their ERP systems, we have up-to-date information from thousands of SAP systems. Panaya's information includes historical behavior with regards to system upgrades and changes, satellite applications at customer sites and more.

By constantly analyzing this data, we can create a trend analysis of the SAP customer's ecosystem behavior overtime, reflecting which versions were adopted and how quickly.

Such an example can be seen in Exhibit 2 outlining which Enhancement Pack (EHP) upgrades were performed by customers at different points in time (X axis), and the percentage of systems on a specific version at a certain point (Y axis).

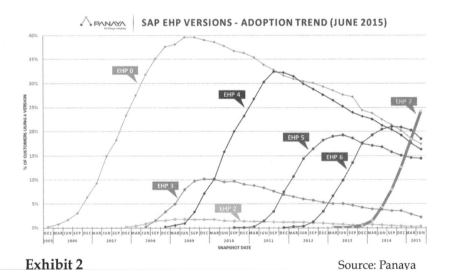

Exhibit 2   Source: Panaya

The following observations can be made from the chart:

- Not all customers adopt every new SAP version. Even the most adopted EHP 4 reached a peak adoption rate of approximately 35 percent, about three years after becoming generally available (GA).

- The time it takes a new version to reach peak adoption is approximately 18–24 months after GA. In addition, we can see that EHP 7 (the latest version, and the required version to support Business Suite on HANA as well as Fiori), has a steeper adoption rate and has the potential to become the most adopted version.

- Unlike Android or mobile applications, the expected upswing in ERP adoption is measured in years and not months. In a different survey, we asked customers why they were adopting EHP 7 and received the responses summarized in Exhibit 3. As you can see, HANA is one of the major reasons but not necessarily *the* top one; however, we see a growing number of customers starting to plan and get ready for such a future move."

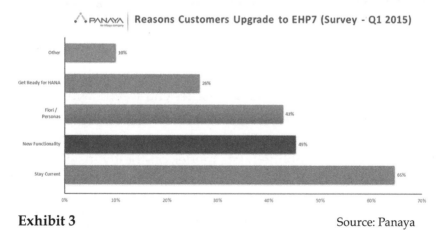

Exhibit 3   Source: Panaya

Still, it was a good omen that there is relatively strong momentum around adoption of EHP 7 and the stage was set for the S/4 launch in New York.

New York S/4 Launch

The event started full of promise, with Dr. Plattner ringing the bell at the New York Stock Exchange. McDermott built expectations with his comment, "This is an historic day and we believe it marks the beginning of the end for the 20th century IT stack and all the complexity that came with it."[16]

McDermott summarized S/4 as follows:

"We had to reinvent that great core (of the previous R/3 product) . . . S stands for simple, 4 for fourth generation, HANA stands for in-memory, real-time, where you can run your entire company, radically simplified at a speed never before achieved, in real-time, in the cloud . . . or on-premise . . . (It's a) game changer."

Dr. Plattner and Bernd Leukert, Executive Board Member for Products and Innovation, tried to demo what the company's website describes as:

"SAP S/4HANA extends the value of simplicity to all lines of business and industries end-to-end with guided configuration for adoption, a modern user experience for business users of all roles in a company on almost any device, a simplified data model, on-the-fly insight at the

---

[16] http://www.news-sap.com/sap-unveils-next-generation-enterprise-software-new-business-suite-sap-s4hana/

highest level of granularity and re-imagined real-time business processes."[17]

On that day in New York, Dr. Plattner and Leukert only had 45 minutes for their presentation. However, they have elaborated their passion for in-memory computing in a 300-page book, *The In-Memory Revolution: How SAP HANA Enables Business of the Future.*[18] The book (with the obligatory disclaimer that it is not "official SAP communication material") describes the genesis of the S/4 product starting back in March 2012 and internal debates at SAP on how best to design a "nondisruptive" next-gen product.

Dr. Plattner says in the book, "You wouldn't believe my prognosed TCO savings, but here are some facts: data entry is three to four times faster, analytics ten to one thousand times faster, the development of extensions much faster, and there is significantly less database administration work, with a data footprint of 1/10 and an unlimited workload capacity via replication."

In nontechnical terms, S/4 should reduce the amount of derived data most companies store today in their enterprise applications, and instead calculate the data in real time as needed, at blazing speeds with today's memory. This reduces storage requirements and also simplifies the data structure and enterprise architecture.

Unfortunately, the lingering image SAP left in New York was that S/4 was essentially a technical upgrade. They might

---

[17] http://www.news-sap.com/sap-unveils-next-generation-enterprise-software-new-business-suite-sap-s4hana/

[18] http://www.amazon.com/-Memory-Revolution-Enables-Business-Future/dp/3319166727/ref=sr_1_1?ie=UTF8&qid=1432042841&sr=8-1&keywords=plattner

well have joked as an industry executive did in the prior decade, "Our software is buzzword-compliant."

Richard Hirsch, a long-time SAP consultant and "SAP Mentor," would remark later:

> "In my opinion, SAP too often associates the fundamental database-related advantages of HANA such as increased speed with the new offer. To a lesser degree, generic cloud-related benefits like subscription-based pricing, quarterly release cycles, etc.. are promoted as well. In my opinion, there needs to be more emphasis placed on the process-related benefits of re-imagining the various modules, especially when integrated with the various other cloud/SaaS assets: Ariba, Fieldglass, Employee Central, etc., that SAP owns."[19]

Tim Fisher of Capgemini, in a column about payback from HANA, has commented:

> "I think it's down to the fact that we've all struggled when the business says 'OK it's quicker . . . but so what?' Up to this point the good answers have been few and far between so the investment decisions simply haven't been made."[20]

The New York event was also light on two key details, product timing and migration paths.

---

[19] http://diginomica.com/2015/05/18/white-boarding-sap-s4-hana/#.VbOh MLNVhBc

[20] https://www.linkedin.com/pulse/whats-going-wrong-business-case-sap-hana-tim-fisher

As Josh Greenbaum of EAConsult put it:

> "SAP needs to make sure every customer understands how the versions of SAP they are running today will lead them to S/4 HANA, in what time frame and at what cost."[21]

During the event, the investment (as against payback) economics were only accented as SAP showcased its larger and longer-term partners which included Accenture, Capgemini, Deloitte Consulting, Ernst & Young and PricewaterhouseCoopers. If anything, the presence of these partners invoked a throwback to the painful, runaway ERP projects of the 1990s.

After the launch, Dr. Plattner commented to a journalist "If this doesn't work, we're dead. Flat-out dead." While that was a brutally honest statement, the event raised questions about whether SAP knew what "this" should be, let alone whether it would work. Defining "this" meant answering the many questions customers and analysts had raised (and which we will explore in detail in the next chapter).

SAP has gradually started to answer those questions on its openSAP courseware[22] and through a series of blog posts and related clarifications. Much of the detail has focused on Simple Finance, Fiori and HANA which are product elements SAP had already been discussing for some time. An eBook[23], with information on how to "deliver real-time business value in the context of your industry" which was supposed to provide

---

[21] http://diginomica.com/2015/02/12/burning-questions-following-sap-s4hana-announcement/#.VbOiYbNVhBc

[22] https://open.sap.com/pages/about

[23] http://global.sap.com/community/ebook/2013_09_27806/enUS/index.html#/page/13

answers to 26 industries, showed links to brochures dated July 2013. That's not exactly "real-time."

The fine print became clearer in later announcements. For example, Simple Logistics will most likely be released in October 2015, but only in a private cloud setting. Rick Sherlund of Nomura reported from his Software Conference on the presentation made by Dr. Rouven Bergmann, former CFO of SAP North America:

> "Dr. Bergmann admitted that Simple Finance will likely remain largely on premise, as the complexity imbedded in the Finance modules of customers is far too complex to simply move the SaaS-based cloud application for Simple Finance. The SaaS-based Simple Finance product will need to be limited in its functionality. The HCM module, however, will more likely be implemented in the public cloud model. Business value will be better generated at the endpoint level."[24]

Rob Enslin, SAP's President of Global Customer Operations would later confirm "Yes, all of the [more than 900 S/4] deals are all on-premise. Our cloud piece for S/4, we're taking it step-by-step for now."[25]

Dr. Plattner added to the mixed messages when soon after the New York launch he blogged, "Since I worked once for IBM, I take announcements very seriously."[26] This was an unfortu-

---

[24] Nomura Quick Note: SAP (SAP GY, Buy)—Nomura Software Conference Takeaways, March 12, 2015

[25] http://www.asugnews.com/article/sap-customer-chief-rob-enslin-whats-really-going-on-with-s-4hana

[26] https://blogs.saphana.com/2015/02/14/freedom-speech-facts-announcement/

nate comment as it brought back images of IBM's reputation for "marketecture" and "freeze the market" announcements.

In parallel, a survey of 120 SAP UK and Ireland User Group members showed that while 63% of those surveyed intend to adopt SAP HANA in the next several years, current take-up was a mere 10 percent.[27]

Another survey by Rimini Street, focusing more on the U.S., indicated that less than 15 percent of SAP customers were convinced they would adopt S/4. Of the total, 68 percent of respondents cited "No strong business case and unclear ROI." Product immaturity was among the many reasons cited by respondents.[28]

The Orlando "Re-launch"

With the cynicism growing, the hope was that SAP would come out blazing with details at its annual SAPPHIRE NOW event in May.

However, something strange happened at the event in Orlando.

McDermott, an eloquent speaker who is recognized as one of the best software salespeople in the world, waited 20 minutes into his kickoff keynote speech to talk about S/4. He joked about the unwieldy product name, and after a few minutes punted it to Leukert to cover the details on the next day. In fairness, McDermott was handicapped by the absence of Sheryl Sandberg, COO of Facebook, who was supposed to have presented with him. Sandberg had to cancel due to the sudden passing of her husband, Dave Goldberg. As a result, McDermott shortened his keynote by 30 minutes. Yet if he had

---

[27] http://diginomica.com/2015/04/21/sap-hana-struggles-for-adoption-in-the-uk/
[28] http://www.riministreet.com/sr-sap-application-strategies-for-2015-and-beyond

chosen to address the new product, there was still plenty of time to devote to S/4. In the future, it may well be called the "S/4 Sounds of Silence" speech.

Maybe we have all been spoiled by Apple product launches, and in particular by Steve Jobs' signature "one more thing" portion of the speech where he usually introduced something spectacular. McDemott's "one more thing" came across as odd. He chose to have his staff demo the Concur (a 2014 SAP acquisition) travel expense management product. Now, travel administration is a nuisance in most companies, but from the largest application vendor in the world you expect bigger initiatives. You would expect from SAP the equivalent of the Boeing Dreamlifter, such as solutions for thorny supply chain management challenges. Or he could have reached into the Plattner/Leukert book where they showcase examples of medical research insights, fraud detection, hurricane damage prediction for insurers and consumer sentiment analysis.

Three years earlier, then co-CEO Jim Hagemann Snabe had told the same audience:

> "Give us the most complicated problem in your business that could not be solved due to lack of speed or volume of data and let's see what we can do. You'll be amazed at the type of problems we can solve."[29]

Most of us are seeing mobile apps from our airlines, hotels, card companies, travel agents and from start-ups like Expensify. The visual of the CEO showcasing an expense management

---

[29] http://www.news-sap.com/ceo-sapphire-now-snabe-cloud-inmemory/#sthash. hGDu8aR0.dpuf

app, while shortchanging S/4—which he had called "historic" just a few weeks prior—was as awkward as SAP showcasing its "fat-cat" partners in New York.

When Leukert, an engineer, was assigned the S/4 sales job in his keynote the next morning, he emphasized that unique functionality for 25 industries would be included in the product release. In New York, Dr. Plattner had initially said only a handful of industries were in its scope. So, had SAP developers been furiously burning the midnight oil to reverse course since February?

Holger Mueller of Constellation Research observed in his First Take commentary:

> "I am worried that SAP overstated the scope and capability of S/4HANA—wondering how all 25 industry code can be available just 3 months after launch. These are millions of lines of code, and to bring them all to the qualities Plattner postulated at the launch 3 months ago seems . . . impossible."[30]

Leukert clarified afterwards in a press Q&A session what he meant by "industry coverage":

> "After the S/4HANA launch the development teams have worked hard to make sure that the 25 industry code 'runs' with S/4HANA. 'Runs' means that the system will not crash, and works, but it is also not optimized for usage of HANA as the database, the products don't

---

[30] http://enswmu.blogspot.com/2015/05/first-take-sapphirenow-bernd-leukert.html

have a Fiori UI, they are not simplified and augmented with modern best practices."[31]

SAP's Enslin would confirm later "When it comes to the cloud option, right now it's limited to service-based companies and to marketing solutions."[32]

You could hardly call that ready-to-deploy functionality. I asked an executive at a flagship customer in one of SAP's major industry groups if he thought it would be ready to move to S/4 by 2020. His response:

> "I think 2020 is too aggressive. SAP's 25 industry groups will massively compete with each other for R&D investment dollars . . ."

This executive may be overly cautious, as many industry groups at SAP have their own dedicated development resources. However, the schema rationalization and code rewrite to use HANA that SAP has showcased around Simple Finance would need to be done around each unique industry-specific functionality.

Or perhaps that executive was merely being realistic. Simon Paris, the well-respected President of the SAP Industry Cloud group, who left soon after the SAPPHIRE conference to become CEO of Misys (a vendor focused on software for banks and other financial services customers) had explained in an interview the SAP industry-specific investment allocation process:

---

[31] http://enswmu.blogspot.com/2015/05/event-report-sap-sapphire-top-3.html
[32] http://www.asugnews.com/article/sap-customer-chief-rob-enslin-whats-really-going-on-with-s-4hana

"Firstly there are the strategic industries. They carry on being strategic in terms of our disproportionate investment in anticipation of disproportionate return. Then our core industries which are the bulk of our revenue and of our maintenance. The customers rightfully expect more industry-specific innovation. And then the third category, which for now we're calling incubation industries, are industries which are relatively small today, but have the potential to be huge. An example of that could be healthcare or sports, media, and entertainment. So those make up the industry clustering within Industry Cloud."[33]

If you parse that statement, SAP is targeting a lot more than 25 industries to cover "micro-verticals" such as sports teams, and the investment allocation process will likely be opportunistic.

Kustoff, the Endo CIO introduced earlier, said:

"I do not expect functionality for my (pharma) industry on S/4HANA to be mature for five years. In fairness I have not seen many specifics from SAP so may consider a different timeline once they articulate greater clarity on their plans."

An enterprise architect with years of SAP experience explained what he thinks he has heard about the new product:

"Is S/4 really simple? Actually, it's probably the reverse. SAP's ERP is made up of tens of thousands of tables that

---

[33] http://www.news-sap.com/simon-paris-industry-cloud/#sthash.w3vUKpPx.dpuf

represent hundreds of thousands of pieces of discrete data. Some of it is real data, some of it is metadata and some of it is configuration data for the system. All of it is designed for SAP's process-centric view of the world.

What SAP has done with S/4 is simplify the underlying structure through database views in HANA. So it's another layer on top of the database that compounds very granular underlying database tables into logical business constructs; something that has always been done by the application logic in SAP (the data in SAP is dumb—all the intelligence is in the logic). And since that SAP logic is all process driven in the "order to cash" or "procure to pay" themes, making business sense of that data can be a real bitch. What it is NOT is a material reduction in tables or a simplification of the data structure. By definition it can't be because those hundreds of million lines of ABAP code all point to those original tables in some way; so until the code is rewritten, the tables still need to exist. And that includes all the customer customizations . . . .

Are these views valuable? Absolutely. They make reporting much easier—less piecing together of widely distributed bits of data from controlling tables, materials tables, etc., that get it in the way of what you really want, not that the ERP systems process design decided you want. And for building custom apps on top of SAP, it's a much simpler POV. But is it actually simpler?

No.

It's another layer on top of the layers that already exist. It is additive. And the more layers, the more issues with context and integrity—and the more challenges in maintaining relationships when the underlying tables change.

Also, though the views are great for getting things out, but they really can't put things back. So it's really analytics only. To put it back in SAP, you have to follow the old rules and it has to go to the original tables.

So, for a shiny new customer engaging with SAP for the first time, S/4 is much more understandable, and customizations and reports will be much easier for them than for those that went before.

But for existing customers, you now have a new metaphor that is separate from the old one. You can build new things more easily. But it doesn't replace what you have done. So you now have to know two things, not one. Plus, for the new one, you have to understand what its capable of. So, for information out its fine, but for inserting or editing, you have to understand that you are dealing with a view, so you have to use the old ways for updating.

So, is it simpler? Depends on where you are in your SAP lifecycle and what you want to do."

Geoff Scott, CEO of the Americas' SAP Users' Group (ASUG), observed succinctly:

"You've taken a 20 TB database and compressed it to 10 TB or 5 TB—I get that. . . But to us, simple is also about faster and easier configuration, getting people up to speed faster and getting changes into production super-fast."[34]

The "Rolling Launch"

Speaking on behalf of the users, Scott could have also pointed out SAP should accelerate S/4 adoption in the customer base. In its 2Q15 earnings report, SAP claimed "more than 900 SAP S/4HANA customers"[35]. Enslin, introduced above, painted a much more realistic picture in his comments: "We have roughly double digit customers live on Simple Finance . . . In total, we have 137 running projects . . . Many are waiting for the full impact of logistics (functionality).'[36]

If you analyze Enslin's comments, the S/4 adoption to date is modest. Simple Finance has been talked about for over a year and you would expect more customers to be live. Logistics functionality will not be available till later this year, and it is not that interesting to many of SAP's customers in banking, services and other industries. Many of the early adopters like Shell are trying out multiple projects—so, the "137 running projects" Enslin mentions are at a small fraction of the 900 plus customers who are supposed to have bought S/4.

After the New York event, the analyst firm Gartner commented:

> "SAP S/4HANA Is a Transformational Shift for SAP and Its Users, but Hold on to Your Wallets for Now . . . . The

---

[34] http://www.cio.com/article/2923193/sap-journeys-to-simplicity-but-customers-still-live-in-a-complex-world.html

[35] http://global.sap.com/corporate-en/investors/newsandreports/news.epx?articleID=24735&category=45

[36] http://diginomica.com/2015/07/21/saps-q2-fy2015-more-color-on-the-results-s4-is-acoming-hana-revived/?#.Va7JAvlVhBc

launch of SAP S/4HANA creates more questions for SAP users than it answers, resulting in road map uncertainty for existing and prospective SAP clients."[37]

Brian Sommer, analyst at TechVentive, added:

"This is a constantly moving target so don't expect the list (of questions) to get any shorter!"[38]

The SAPPHIRE event in Orlando, three months later, did not shorten the list of questions and it looked like SAP would have to keep clarifying the scope of S/4. When you are dealing with complex enterprise software that is not totally unexpected, but it sounded more like a "rolling launch" where the final shape of S/4 would not be known for months, or even years.

In the next chapter, we will look at many of the questions that SAP will need to address as the S/4 rollout continues to unfold.

---

[37] https://www.gartner.com/doc/2991820/sap-shana-transformational-shift-sap
[38] http://diginomica.com/2015/02/12/burning-questions-following-sap-s4hana-announcement/#.VbOqr7NVhBc

CHAPTER 3

As Simple as Possible, But Not Simpler

⋏⋏➔

Albert Einstein has been credited with the enigmatic quote of "Everything Should Be Made as Simple as Possible, But Not Simpler." In keeping with its new "Run Simple" branding, perhaps SAP was trying to keep the S/4HANA messaging simple. This chapter will explore the many questions that still need answering.

When will SAP catch up to functionality that reflects dramatic changes in every industry?
S/4 should ideally make up for its predecessor, Business Suite, which has been lagging in functionality for years now. SAP has missed out on next-gen factory and supply chain innovations, which in its native Germany have generated excitement under the moniker of *Industrie 4.0*. Moreover, its CRM functionality has not kept up with social and digital marketing innovations and

it has missed out on telematics innovations that are reshaping insurance, mobile innovations that are reshaping banking and numerous innovations in every industry it services.

In *SAP Nation*, Andre Blumberg, Director of IT at CLP Group, a showcase Asia-Pacific utility for SAP, had commented:

> "Mobile enterprise application platform, predictive maintenance, emission management, work clearance, safety document management and advanced analytics opportunities were awarded to other vendors. Fuel and commodity management functionality was custom developed."

Lora Cecere, a respected supply chain management analyst, summarized what you could say about SAP functionality in many industries:

> "When SAP launched APO in 2002, the optimization technologies were inferior to most best-of-breed technologies in the market. Over the years, as technology innovation has improved, staying current on supply chain planning optimization has not been a focus for SAP. Relative to other technology development areas, the opportunity for SAP was not as great. They quickly became a market leader and then shifted resources to other areas.
>
> As a result, the most successful SAP Supply Chain Planning implementations layer on optimization technology (is) from a specialist vendor or University. It is an expensive workaround."[39]

---

[39] http://www.supplychainshaman.com/uncategorized/three-reasons-why-sap-is-a-risk/

As Cecere says in the comments above, several customers have been "ring fencing" SAP with specialist solutions. HP, one of SAP's largest customers (and partners), has been doing so in many of its customer-facing systems and the systems to support that transformation will make HP the largest Salesforce implementation in the world. It also boasts some of the largest Workday (for HR functions), Fieldglass (for contract labor procurement) and DocuSign (for electronic contracts) implementations.

HP is also using E2open for Order Promising and Response Planning, as well as deploying its Supply Chain Planning to synch components from suppliers with its contract manufacturers and HP's Software unit has been implementing NetSuite.

S/4, as initially presented, comes across as yet another technical upgrade—speedier in some scenarios, prettier with the Fiori UX in others, but hardly a giant leap in major functionality.

The Plattner/Leukert book quotes:

> "To move from R/2 to R/3 was huge; the move to S/4HANA has many more benefits."

The systems architect quoted in the previous chapter challenges that assertion with:

> "Is it really the "4" to R/3? Yeah. But is 4 the fabled unicorn that 3 was to R/2? No."

When will SAP environments be truly "simplified"?

As part of its S/4 launch, SAP has amplified its "simplification" talk and it is imploring customers to "move back to standard," and replace ABAP customizations with extensions in its HANA cloud platform.

This in turn has led to speculation in the developer community about SAP giving up on ABAP.

Jelena Perfiljeva, a respected SAP practitioner, commented on SCN:

> "Cloud means "no ABAP" + SAP wants everyone in the Cloud = SAP wants "no ABAP." So when SAP says "no, ABAP is still alive" it actually makes the paranoid types like me even more suspicious. Clearly SAP is just making sure us ABAPers don't escape from the asylum too quickly and leave their customers stranded."[40]

SAP has promised "guided configurations" with S/4 to streamline parameter setup. That may work with new customers—maybe. Earlier customers did not customize R/3 for the fun of it. They did it because SAP functionality was lacking in many areas. Dan Aldridge colorfully described the predicament many SAP customers faced:

> "To SAP ERP customers, it was as if they had bought a Millennium Falcon back in the '90s and it was being (semi) mothballed in the 2000's. They couldn't upgrade to the latest Jedi fighter because the cost and pain of retrofitting was (potentially) high. So they stuck to their Millennium Falcons and applied duct tape."[41]

So, is it not likely new customers will find similar gaps, given that SAP has not been growing much in functionality during

---

[40] http://scn.sap.com/community/abap/blog/2015/05/29/i-just-heard-sap-are-trying-to-kill-abap-once-again

[41] https://www.linkedin.com/pulse/sap-erp-customers-may-force-you-aldridge-twitter-danaldridge1-?trk=prof-post

the last decade? SAP's desire to reduce ABAP customizations is timely, even critical. Paikowsky of Panaya, introduced earlier talks about their analysis of customer code (and as Exhibit 1 illustrates):

> "Our data shows approximately 50 percent of customers use 60 percent or less of their custom code. Being able to easily identify which parts of that code can be safely cleaned from the system can help reduce the future cost of such upgrades."

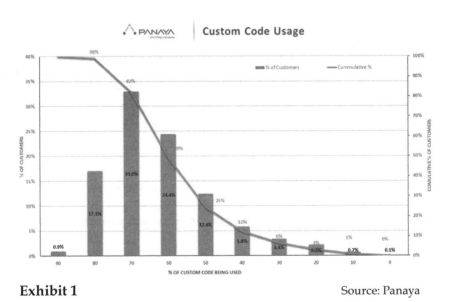

Exhibit 1   Source: Panaya

CAST Research Labs focuses on empirical studies of software implementation in business technology. Earlier this year, CAST benchmarked ABAP applications at large SAP customers—78 ABAP applications consisting of 48 million lines of code (MLOC). The size of these applications was spread widely, with several consisting of more than 2 MLOC. They measured structural quality on robustness, performance, security, change-ability and transferability. As the CAST report reads: "Scores for these measures are computed on a scale of 1 (high risk) to 4 (low risk) by analyzing the application to detect violations of over 1,200 good architectural and coding practices. Scoring is based on an algorithm that evaluates the number of times a violation occurred compared to the number of opportunities where it could have occurred, weighted by the severity of the violation and its relevance to each individual quality characteristic."[42]

A couple of things stood out in the SAP sample compared to others in the CAST database:

- The mean of 615 KLOC is larger than observed for the mean size for other CAST samples.

- The number and density of violations is high in every health factor.

As *Information Age* reported, "With the exception of security, at least 25% of the scores for all of CAST's quality factors fell below 3.0—a staggering number of applications which are currently highly vulnerable."[43]

So, it may be time for SAP and its customers to revisit ABAP customizations, especially the larger ones. But where to move them? SAP needs to offer to make them part of the core, and it needs to help automate the migration either to the core or to extensions in the HANA cloud platform.

---

[42] CAST Research on Application Software Health (CRASH) Benchmark Report 2015 – SAP
[43] http://www.information-age.com/industry/software/123459540/theres-no-easy-way-say-sap-not-simple

Until that happens, it will mean expensive, labor-intensive conversion projects.

Charlie Bess, formerly of EDS/HP, knows quite a bit about outsourcing. Walking around the booths at SAPPHIRE, he noticed the large number of "facilitators" and commented:

> "One measurement to watch over time is the mix and background of the attendees. If the utilization is truly becoming simple there will be fewer facilitators and more people with money to spend and value to generate directly in the business."[44]

While Bess was observing partner booths at SAPPHIRE, customers have been complaining that SAP's own support has progressively gotten worse, even around the core SAP product.

Nicolas Busson, an active participant in the SCN community, summarized in a post: "It's just that sometimes I feel like we need to write the same kind of post every month to be heard."[45]

Busson was referring to standard Business Suite support. In a growing SAP world with customizations, acquired software companies and cloud wrinkles, the support issues have become exponentially more complex. In the Rimini Street survey cited in the previous chapter, customers outlined the top three issues they had with SAP-provided support and maintenance:

---

[44] https://cebess.wordpress.com/2015/05/07/measuring-simple-in-a-conference-like-sapphirenow/?fb_action_ids=10205590479814953&fb_action_types=news.publishes&fb_ref=pub-standard&fb_source=other_multiline&action_object_map=%5B784640994984960%5D&action_type_map=%5B%22news.publishes%22%5D&action_ref_map=%5B%22pub-standard%22%5D
[45] http://scn.sap.com/community/software-support-and-maintenance/blog/2015/06/10/just-for-fun-a-day-in-my-life

- Too expensive for number of support calls. (46 percent)
- Too expensive for new functionality delivered. (37 percent)
- No support for customizations. (35 percent)

When will the SAP cloud become world-class?

In *SAP Nation*, I had described the cost, speed and other advantages cloud vendors like Salesforce, Workday, NetSuite and Plex have brought to enterprise software. With S/4, SAP started to promise the benefits of its own public cloud, including more rapid (up to four) releases a year.

While SAP has invested over $20 billion in acquiring public cloud vendors like SuccessFactors, Ariba, Concur and Fieldglass, it has shown a split personality about public clouds. Albert Pang had reported at the previous SAPPHIRE:

> "During a Q&A session, SAP chairman Hasso Plattner dismissed the benefits of multi-tenant delivery of its enterprise applications, primarily those that deal with mission-critical functions like supply chain and financials. Plattner recalled a heated debate over the merits of multi-tenancy with Lars Dalgaard of SuccessFactors after it was bought by SAP in 2012. To this date, Plattner's position, though not unique, remains that SAP's biggest customers—fearing unnecessary business disruption—would still prefer deploying their applications either in a private cloud setting or as managed services, all without the intrusion of continuous updates commonly found in other Cloud applications."[46]

---

[46] http://www.appsruntheworld.com/opinions/index/143#sthash.oOOAxgrt.dpuf

Richard Hirsch reported from the recent SAPPHIRE that Dr. Plattner may indeed be reading his customers correctly:

> "Thus, most of the initial S/4 HANA customers (there are over 400) are using the product in a "private" setting rather than a "public" setting. Indeed, I have yet to hear of a customer running one of three S/4 HANA editions in the public cloud."[47]

SAP says that count of 400 S/4 customers grew to over 900 by the end of the second quarter of 2015. It is fair to note here that in spite of SAP's constant reminders that it is a "system of record" for its customers, there is considerable cynicism in the analyst world about SAP's own reporting of customer and user counts. There is speculation about what exactly the 900 customers who are claimed as S/4 customers may have actually contracted, as the product is relatively new. Some think previous customers of Business Suite on HANA may be part of this number.

It is not uncommon for software vendors (not just SAP, but also Oracle, IBM and others) to heavily incent the sales field to bring in new product revenues, especially as they strive to report more cloud revenues to Wall Street. Most customers tend to discount such counts and find that conversations with peers who have experience with new products is far better validation. Some customers have learned the hard way that the discounts for early adoption of new products often just leads to "shelfware," and later attempts to trade or renegotiate licenses are very messy.

The reality is that many SAP customers are moving from traditional hosting providers like HP and IBM to what the research firm, Forrester, calls "hosted private clouds," using

---

[47] http://diginomica.com/2015/05/18/white-boarding-sap-s4-hana/

vendors like Virtustream (recently acquired by EMC) and Datapipe. With virtualized platforms, they are somewhat more economical (compared to previous hosting arrangements) and, importantly, allow customers to continue with their previously discussed customizations.

However, Forrester has cautioned about private clouds:

> "Cloud by definition should be a standardized set of IT resources. Although public clouds standardize resources across all customers, this is not a safe assumption for hosted private. Some hosted private cloud providers center their business on creating private cloud environments built on custom hardware with custom contracts for their users, thus becoming more of a private cloud that is managed and hosted by a third party, rather than a standardized cloud service with segmentation between users. Pricing, contract length and time-to-delivery are largely tied to the level of customization available for customers. Customers that view hosted private as an alternative to private cloud like additional customizations, whereas those focused on a more secure public cloud option should look to the more standardized offerings."[48]

While private clouds will bring some virtualization efficiencies, they will only scratch the surface of the massive offshore application management and the upgrade project economics and risks that have become the hallmark of on-premise SAP implementations.

---

[48] https://www.forrester.com/The+Forrester+Wave+Hosted+Private+Cloud+Solutions+Q4+2014/fulltext/-/E-RES113725

There is another concern about SAP's S/4 public cloud. The data center, in Sankt Leon-Rot, Germany, while close to SAP's impressive Walldorf headquarters, does not itself inspire much confidence. It has been called "puny and primitive" compared to the data centers of infrastructure-as-a-service providers like Amazon, Microsoft Azure and Rackspace. Indeed, competitors like Infor and Unit4 are using infrastructure-as-a-service (using data centers from Amazon and Microsoft, respectively) rather than try to compete with their scale. Oracle has invested in its own formidable string of global data centers to be competitive with Amazon and other cloud infrastructure providers. Additionally, given SAP's tendency to prefer partnering over building, it is likely even the "public cloud" could end up getting spread across many of its hosting and other outsourcing partners. In that scenario, you could potentially end up with even more of the inconsistencies that Forrester has described.

Even where SAP offers public cloud options—for example with its SuccessFactors and Concur customers—the individual data centers are undersized and often supported by co-location vendors around the globe. SAP's "about 82 million cloud users"[49] are fragmented across products and across geographies. Little attempt appears to have been made, to date, to consolidate data centers that support them. While compliance requirements dictate regional diversity in such facilities, they are further reminders of Balkanization in the SAP economy.

SAP's acquired cloud products also face many competitive challenges as they try to accelerate growth.

---

[49] http://seekingalpha.com/article/3342475-sap-ags-sap-ceo-bill-mcdermott-on-q2-2015-results-earnings-call-transcript?page=2

Gartner has already anointed the "Big Three" when it comes to cloud HCM, and it describes the dog fight experienced by SuccessFactors even when trying to protect on-premise SAP HCM customers:

> "All upper midmarket (more than 2,500 employees) and large global enterprises (more than 10,000 employees in multiple regions) need to manage their human capital management (HCM) application portfolio strategically . . . However, technology evaluations executing the developed strategy conducted by organizations in this size range will almost always include at least an initial assessment of the HCM cloud solutions offered by Oracle, SAP and Workday. As the selection process continues, Gartner client inquiry reveals that it is also likely that one or two of the three will be identified as finalist vendors."[50]

While SAP reports that it can help Concur (with its T&E services) grow faster in global markets, Concur increasingly competes with various travel sites and mobile applications, and faces increased competition from similar offerings of other ERP vendors.

The Ariba and Fieldglass business models face their own pressures, as this comment on the Spend Matters site summarizes: "The 'supplier pays' model is hugely flawed in our view as well. It hinders adoption and it is akin to blackmail (give us money else you won't get paid!). If both parties received tangible value from the product, then it would be fair to make both pay,

---

[50] https://www.gartner.com/doc/3046126?ref=SiteSearch&sthkw=hanscome&fnl=search&srcId=1-3478922254

otherwise just the one side should. Inevitably, if we were a supplier on such systems, I would increase my pricing to account for the invoice fee. So, who is paying then? The buyer. Twice."[51]

Customers also report that SAP's recent software economics (as against business network economics described above) are uncompetitive whether it is proposing on-premise or its cloud solutions. For example, in a recent deal, its five-year software cost was three times as much as the winning competitor cloud bid. SAP's annual maintenance cost by itself exceeded the subscription cost of the competition, which also included hosting, apps management and upgrades in its price.

How do we mitigate the risks of adopting HANA as a transaction database?

The cornerstone of S/4 is SAP's in-memory, columnar database, HANA. In recent years, SAP has been pushing HANA, and many of its customers have been evaluating it as an analytics engine. While SAP claims over 7,000 customers have adopted it (2 percent of its total customer base), others such as GE have pursued a radically different "data lakes" direction. Still others have adopted the open source, Big Data platform Hadoop, or found that lighter tools such as Sisense are adequate for their needs.

HANA as a transaction processing platform, however, is something about which customers are a bit more nervous. Some customers have tried it in low-risk "sidecar" projects, while many others report reservations about HANA.

---

[51] https://spendmatters.com/2012/12/21/ariba-doesnt-have-customers-it-has-prisoners/

R/3 (now Business Suite) avoided database-specific features like stored procedures. This allowed customers database portability choices. In fact, that was SAP's rallying cry for over two decades. But with S/4, SAP is reversing direction and is moving logic from the application layer into the HANA database.

Dr. Plattner defended that move as a way to simplify the code. In a comment to a blog post, he said:

> "That R/3 didn't use stored procedures is true. The sERP version of the suite on HANA not only dropped the transactionally maintained aggregates and all redundant materialized views, but heavily uses stored procedures and other libraries of the HANA platform. The application code is being simplified dramatically. The transactional performance increases accordingly."[52]

So one of the more controversial moves with S/4 is a de-emphasis of that two-decades-old SAP commitment to database portability. As John Appleby of Bluefin Solutions (recently acquired by Mindtree) said emphatically:

> "Since the announcement of SAP S/4HANA in February 2015, it has become clear that HANA is the only first-class citizen."[53]

For SAP and its partners that statement may ring true, but not to many of its customers. P. J. Jakovljevic, Principal Analyst

---

[52] https://blogs.saphana.com/2014/08/29/the-benefits-of-the-business-suite-on-hana/
[53] Building the business case for SAP HANA; Appleby, John; a Bluefin Solutions publication, 2015

at Technology Evaluation Centers, wrote in his Product Note on S/4:

> "There is no longer a need for the so-called materialized views (i.e., a layer of snapshots of aggregates, totals, and other redundant data) that Oracle, Microsoft SQL Server, IBM DB2, and other supported databases have traditionally needed as a layer. This means incredible speed and simplicity, but will legacy SAP customers move from Oracle or SQL Server, and will they appreciate the lack of database choice?"[54]

While simplification is a good end result, many customers express an obvious concern about increased lock-in by SAP. Other customers express caution about the still-emerging systems management discipline around HANA. David Cooper, CIO at British Gas, told me when I interviewed him for *SAP Nation*:

> "HANA would have to match [current] resilience and disaster recovery thresholds needed for heavy transaction processing. When considering the business case for HANA, the years of experience in the team working with the Oracle database and the cost of retraining need to be considered . . . we do not have a burning performance problem today to justify the risks of moving to HANA as a transaction engine."

---

[54] http://www.technologyevaluation.com/research/TEC-report/The-Biggest-SAP-Product-Launch-in-a-Quarter-Century-and-What-it-Means-to-ERP.html

Another executive commented:

> "SAP appears to have forgotten there are huge back-end CA and HP APM [performance management and monitoring] systems tracking every server and DBA that companies have large NOCs monitoring everything."

It has not helped matters that SAP has been opaque about HANA benchmarks. For two decades, its SD benchmark, which measures SAP customer order lines processed in its Sales and Distribution (SD) module, has been the gold standard for measuring new hardware and software infrastructure. It has not released those metrics using a HANA database. One of the (unsatisfactory) excuses offered is that the expensive hardware needed to support such a test in a lab is better shipped to paying customers.

Appleby is not that worried about hardware scalability:

> "The answer for the SAP Business Suite is simple right now: you have to scale-up. This advice might change in future, but even an 8-socket 6TB system will fit 95% of SAP customers, and the biggest Business Suite installations in the world can fit in a SGI 32-socket with 24TB—and that's before considering Simple Finance or Data Aging, both of which decrease memory footprint dramatically."[55]

How expensive is that hardware?
"Stupid question," responded an SAP partner to that question. "Budget has never been an issue in SAP shops."

---

[55] https://blogs.saphana.com/2014/12/10/sap-hana-scale-scale-hardware/

Well, OK!

Dr. Plattner has gone further in suggesting customers are too risk averse:

> "That's because we were wimps and thought we'd go the easy way and do the read-only [analytical] applications first."[56]

But even he is sympathetic:

> "I've been working on this for seven and a half years, so I underestimate how much you have to reset your brain to understand the possibilities."

In the meantime, database players like Oracle and Microsoft are offering their own in-memory switches while supporting the systems management and IT talent infrastructure most CIOs have built over the last few decades. So, in a couple of years SAP may have to reverse course about database portability. SAP has already shared dates for continued support of the Oracle Database 12c in-memory switch and its Engineered Systems products like Exadata and the SPARC SuperCluster.

Will Fiori be able to keep up with rapid advances in UX design and expectations?

One of the nicest things to come out of SAP in recent years is its Fiori user experience (UX). In a conversation, Anne Kathrine Petterøe, a long-term SAP practitioner and now a consultant with EVRY, a leading Norwegian services firm, raved about the UX:

---

[56] http://www.informationweek.com/cloud/software-as-a-service/sap-chairman-hasso-plattner-exclusive-qanda/d/d-id/1269486

"With Fiori, it is the first time that I see customers coming to us and asking for a product. Customers have seen demos or heard about it at SAP events and like what they see. There seems to be an understanding now at top management level/strategic level, that the users would like a better/easier user interface for their SAP applications, that I haven't seen before.

We are going live with the Fiori Travel & Expense app for a customer this week, and we see that there isn't a need for training or retraining of end users at all! They intuitively understand the app. I don't think I have ever seen that happen before with SAP software."

Given SAP's notoriously poor UX in the past, you can now see pent-up user demand for the new front end. SAP has invested in creative spaces—each of which is called an AppHaus—in locations like Palo Alto, California and Heidelberg, Germany. There it facilitates customer workshops and co-innovation projects around the new UX.

However, the world of UX is evolving very rapidly. In the last few months I have had a chance to visit the Oracle UX design lab, talk to Infor's in-house design agency Hook & Loop and see Unit4's "self-driving ERP" which leverages Microsoft machine learning. I also have had an opportunity to see a fabulous Microsoft demo that pulled together Skype for Business, Cortana's voice-based personal assistant, Surface Hub display, machine learning via Delve and a variety of Apple and Microsoft mobile hardware.

UX in enterprise software is going through a revolution. Consumer tech UX is moving faster and even Apple finds itself lagging:

> "This year's WWDC was a tacit admission that Apple needed to play catch-up. Cupertino spent so much energy over the past five years paying attention to the surface details of their products, it ignored a seismic shift in the industry: AI is the new UI."[57]

John Underkoffler, who designed the gesture-based interface in the movie *Minority Report* and is now CEO of Oblong Industries, a design studio, has said:

> "We're a digital species now—nothing short of apocalypse will change that! The health of our digital society lies, therefore, in the broadest possible distribution of agency. Agency is circumscribed mainly by the UI—the machinery through which human intent is transduced into the machine. So designing and deploying radically more capable UIs is one of the most important things we can do today."[58]

Fiori is a major step forward when compared to current SAP UX, but if even Apple is having to leapfrog, can SAP and other enterprise vendors afford to be far behind?

The UX challenge amplifies the "Sunday night/Monday morning" phenomenon I have written about in earlier books:

---

[57] http://www.fastcodesign.com/3047199/apple-finally-learns-ai-is-the-new-ui
[58] http://www.fastcompany.com/person/john-underkoffler

What users expect at work should not trail what they are already seeing in their cars and homes. Or at the movies. The trend of "consumerization of technology" will not slow down any time soon. We are seeing radical new UX in the form of voice, gestural, haptic and other interfaces in our cars and home devices.

Petterøe also points out the AppHaus concept can only be used today by customers who can travel to places like Palo Alto or Heidelberg:

> "Working in a smaller region, I wish there was more partner support for Fiori projects, at least now in the beginning when everything is new. We don't have an AppHaus we can take our customers to, to do UX workshops. So mostly the partners are left alone figuring out how to best deliver Fiori projects. Given that the technology is still new, there are a lot of questions coming up, and it is difficult to know to whom we can raise these questions."

What are the economics of moving to S/4?

At the New York launch, Dr. Plattner confidently announced that with S/4:

> "The total cost of ownership goes down, the response time improves and flexibility increases."

Various SAP executives harped on the simplification mantra and again predicted lower TCO as a result.

It's not clear how they can say that, when SAP's own pricing information about S/4 started off rather fuzzy:

> "For the on-premise version, SAP Business Suite customers need to purchase the SAP S/4HANA foundation-promotion license to run the new SAP S/4HANA code line."

and

> "For the cloud, the pricing model will be subscription-based and communicated at a later stage. Please contact your local sales representative for more information."

What exactly is the foundation-promotion license? Chris Kanaracus of ASUG got a clarification from SAP:

> "On-premise customers need to move their Business Suite to SAP HANA and then implement the latest exchange innovation package which brings the new S/4HANA coding . . . . These packages can only be installed by customers having licensed the S/4HANA foundation."[59]

Simple pricing, right?

What about surround costs? In *SAP Nation*, my model showed the majority of the $204 billion annual run rate came from SAP partners and SAP-related staffing observed at customers sites. Will S/4 reduce this annual run rate? If anything, the initial migration costs are likely to be substantial till SAP and its partners develop more automated tools for the data and

---

[59] http://www.asugnews.com/article/sap-s-4hana-faq-pricing-and-licensing-implications

code conversion, end user retraining, testing and other steps in a migration.

Kustoff, the Endo CIO introduced earlier, told me:

> "I have had conversations with senior SAP executives and told them we would like to commit much deeper to HANA. But the total package—the cost of the infrastructure, the cost of migration, etc.—has to be much more financially attractive than it is today."

SAP has been honing its value-engineering expertise over the last decade:

> "SAP offers a proven methodology and approach— for example, design thinking—to help you discover customer-specific business improvement areas and quantify value potential. Our value experts support over 2,000 customers annually using this knowledge base, on topics such as business case building, performance benchmarking and industry best practices."[60]

Many of SAP's payback scenarios, however, play up the *time* dimension more than the financial one:

> "Long-running transactions and overnight batch processing are things of the past because the solution can eliminate latency in data movement by unifying the data store in a single platform. By unifying transactional and analytical processing on a single real-time platform, you can now couple transactions with analysis in real time in

---

[60] http://global.sap.com/community/ebook/2013_09_27806/enUS/index.html#/page/13

a single blended environment to get live insight about a fast-breaking situation. You can dramatically accelerate core business processes and evolve toward supporting real-time scenarios."[61]

and

"Material requirements planning no longer runs overnight, but in real time. This means bottlenecks can be identified faster and warehouse space can be reduced. Additionally, planning is in a position to take all production locations and external supply chains into account. A safety buffer in the warehouses is unavoidable. However, simulations and evaluations help manage capacities and quantities in a much more needs-based way than before—and, thanks to the simplified data model and real-time information from SAP S/4HANA, this happens across all departments and business processes in finance, sales and distribution, and retail sales."[62]

That is certainly appealing until you realize that this is not the SAP system of yesteryear. Today, it is surrounded by many satellite applications and customizations that make the single real-time platform an unrealistic proposition for many customers.

An additional caution for SAP customers is that the last wave of value engineering and business cases that SAP and its partners developed were essentially self-serving. There

---

[61] http://global.sap.com/community/ebook/2013_09_27806/enUS/index.html#/page/13

[62] http://www.news-sap.com/sap-s4hana-six-important-scenarios/#sthash.DJrPQEug.dpuf

have not been many formal postmortems of those ROI justifications. This time around customers may have to rely on their peers for somewhat believable TCO and ROI studies. Specific to S/4 it may take some time before such conversations are possible.

What will SAP do about all the sprawl?

In Chapter 1 we looked at the sprawl in SAP's product portfolio, in satellite apps, customizations in its customer base and in an ever-growing ecosystem.

Statements like this one, from May 2015, are all too common:

> "SAP S/4HANA, cloud edition does not replace our existing portfolio of line-of-business cloud solutions; it will integrate with and expand it. Our comprehensive offering is planned to allow SAP S/4HANA customers to build hybrid scenarios between SAP S/4HANA and cloud solutions from SAP, including those from SuccessFactors, Ariba, SAP hybris Marketing, Fieldglass and SAP JAM."[63]

SAP may need to use its own inventory management system to manage its exploding list of SKUs. Customers complain that few of these products have been integrated to the core Business Suite, let alone with each other.

S/4 as initially defined may only be aimed at less than 10 percent of SAP's customer base on ECC and Business Suite

---

[63] http://www.sapevents.edgesuite.net/s4hana/pdfs/SAPS4HANA%20cloudedition%20ExternalFAQMay2015.pdf

versions. A next-gen product should have something for a larger portion of the customer base. Ideally, S/4 should attempt to rationalize the sprawl in the SAP customer base and provide a path forward for a broader base of customers.

Grading S/4

S/4 is clearly a work in progress, but I have attempted to grade the offering against incumbent SAP technology and those from SAP competitors in Exhibit 2 below:

S/4HANA as initially announced	Compared to		
	SAP existing	Industry	
HANA for analytics	A	B	HANA has matured over five years to be attractive to many SAP customers, but there are several other in-memory, Big Data tools which are less expensive or can scale more.
HANA for trans proc	C	C	No rigorous TP benchmarking yet, insufficient systems management tools around HANA. Also risk of lock-in since S/4 does not support other DB.
Fiori UX	A	B	Compared to existing SAP UX, Fiori is a definite improvement. Compared to evolving UX trends Fiori is already dated.
Cloud Computing	B	C	Private clouds offer improvements compared to current hosting models in SAP shops. But still significantly inefficient compared to public clouds of other vendors.
Functionality			
Financials	A-	B	Simple Finance should be attractive to SAP customers who are prepared to "decompose" their integrated ERP model. However, there are many other financial module choices in marketplace today.
Other ERP	B	B+	Availability of Simple Logistics and other functionality is still unknown. When available they will likely face less market competition than Simple Finance.
Verticals	B	C	Availability of vertical functionality is still unknown. For many industries, unless SAP enhances functionality in S/4, will be lagging
Economics	C	D	Migration costs to S/4 could be unattractive. Ongoing costs will continue to be unattractive compared to alternatives in market

Exhibit 2   Source: Deal Architect

NetWeaver Redux?

With so many unanswered questions, an emerging viewpoint is that S/4, as initially defined, is just a placeholder. If anything, it will probably evolve in the same manner as another of SAP's initiatives, NetWeaver, did a decade ago. In their 2004 book on NetWeaver, Dan Woods and Jeff Word said with confidence:

> "All this talk about successive versions and incremental progress and fulfilling visions could easily give you the wrong impression that SAP NetWeaver is still on the drawing board. That's not at all true. SAP NetWeaver is here now. All the SAP NetWeaver components that we have mentioned are working products and can be purchased and used to make your business run better today."[64]

NetWeaver, introduced as a middleware integration play, evolved over the years into an umbrella for many SAP tools and solutions.

George Anderson, in the 2011 edition of his book on NetWeaver,[65] commented:

> "SAP NetWeaver provides the foundation for Business Suite. But many specific products fall under the label of NetWeaver, too. The NetWeaver umbrella has become so crowded in the past few years that SAP finally organized

---

[64] http://www.amazon.com/SAP-NetWeaver-Dummies-Dan-Woods/dp/07645 68833/ref=sr_1_1?s=books&ie=UTF8&qid=1433509510&sr=1-1&keywords=netwe aver+for+dummies

[65] https://www.amazon.com/gp/r.html?C=O5ID2HJ90BI3&K=A1U7C5QNYFVS Q2&R=ZXC9JVVA9PUX&T=C&U=http%3A%2F%2Fwww.amazon.com%2Fdp%2F B0054XW4LQ%2Fref%3Dpe_385040_118058080_TE_M1T1DP&A=JLSN3Y9AANS VUQZZAGX3ALADWG4A&H=5IVAPGZHFPQKD884WYNHGAJGX9YA

this portfolio of applications, utilities, and tools around six areas (sometimes called domains or themes):

- Foundation management.

- Middleware.

- Information management.

- Team productivity.

- Composition.

- Business Process Management."

S/4 may similarly evolve like NetWeaver over the next few years. As we will see in the next chapter, that is the path many next-gen enterprise software projects have taken over the last two decades.

CHAPTER 4

Mission Accomplished

∿→

Ray Wang of Constellation Research Group interviewed Steve Miranda, SVP Applications Development at Oracle,
to discuss the state of Oracle Fusion cloud applications. Wang
brought up the topic of a "Half Way to Fusion" event Oracle
hosted in downtown San Francisco in January 2006:[66]

> "RW: Let's flash back 7 years ago when Oracle Fusion
> Applications was announced with great fanfare at City
> Hall. You were "half-way"; what's the back story?
>
> SM: Today, we laugh about it, but in all seriousness, we
> started the clock too early. When we acquired PeopleSoft,
> we had a release of Oracle E-Business Suite (EBS). Then,
> we bought BEA, Siebel and Hyperion. Each acquisition
> changed the targets.

---

[66] http://blog.softwareinsider.org/2012/12/31/market-maker-11-steve-miranda-
oracle-fusion-applications-update-the-inside-story/

RW: So you basically underestimated how much work it'd take?

SM: To be blunt, yes."

If Wang had waited a couple of years, he likely would have seen Miranda host a number of his Fusion customers at a different Oracle event. As I wrote in October 2014:

> (Miranda) had executives on stage from BG Group, Marriott, atradius and GE. They represented complex and global challenges—GE is rationalizing over 100 ERP instances from Oracle and others, Marriott talked about social interaction with over 47 million loyalty members, atradius manages collections of over a billion in worldwide debt for its 14,500 global customers, BG Group has HR shared services across 20 countries. And in different ways they discussed speed—GE put in Fusion financials in Mexico in 48 days, Marriott has cut in half social data ingestion time it used to take its agencies with significantly better data quality and atradius talked about a rapid three month SFA project.[67]

Wang and Miranda had been discussing the 2006 Oracle event, which in the enterprise software market is considered the equivalent of the "Mission Accomplished" speech. Yes, it was the one about the Iraq war that U.S. President George W. Bush delivered on an aircraft carrier in May 2003.

Both were premature proclamations of success.

---

[67] https://www.enterpriseirregulars.com/78228/oracles-modern-apps/

The Oracle Fusion Experience

Floyd Teter has a front row seat for the evolution of Fusion, first as a customer, and now as a consultant. He is also a respected member of the Oracle ecosystem as an ACE Director and active participant in the Oracle Applications User Group (OAUG) and the Independent Oracle Users Group (IOUG). Because of his influential role, Oracle has given Teter sneak previews of Fusion as it evolved.

In a conversation, Teter observed:

> "I was really excited about Fusion right from the early days. I liked the user experience. You needed only a few clicks to get to the information you were seeking. It was built around familiar tools—browsers, Microsoft Office, etc. It leveraged Oracle's platform and tools.
>
> But it had a complex technical footprint, especially in terms of supporting middleware. There were plenty of moving parts that projected difficult and expensive (hardware and service dollars) implementations. You could see it was not ready for global release. I found it weak in international regulatory compliance and currency support. The error messages were Greek to functional users. The Oracle sales organization was not well trained on the product and was hesitant to sell it, preferring to sell the incumbent EBS, PeopleSoft and other products."

John Sumser is the founder, principal author and editor-in-chief of the *HRExaminer* online magazine where he explores the people, technology, ideas and careers of senior leaders in human resources and human capital. He also had a keen interest in how Fusion would evolve and be positioned with respect to Oracle's PeopleSoft, Taleo and other HR customer bases.

In an interview, Sumser told me:

"My sense is that Fusion required a bottoms-up design. By starting with what was already in place and re-architecting, they've built a sturdy foundation. You can't learn the things that are necessary lessons by simply announcing a new tool or architecture. Development and launch are just starting points. Enterprise tools don't achieve full utility until they have been used for a while.

Making something like Fusion viable is like seasoning a cast iron skillet. Usage makes it better. It's as if there were an equivalent of Malcolm Gladwell's 10,000 hours for enterprise software and the ecosystems that surround it. The stuff gets better because people use it. Errors are discovered through broad usage. The more time the tool is in the field, the fewer errors a user experiences. While every legitimate piece of code is tested thoroughly, the actual user experience is theoretical until people actually use the tool.

Like consumer products, enterprise endeavors are never any good at the version 1.0 point. In all markets, early adopters carry products for the time where they are less than perfectly useful. "Viability" comes after the product is good enough for people who are not early adopters.

In the Apple universe, early adopters are called fanboys. In enterprise markets, they are loyal customers and people seeking a competitive advantage. People who join the parade early gain significant value, but it comes at the price of some operational inconvenience.

Birthing something like Fusion, that involves a rear-rangement and reorganization of the entire business, naturally took time to mature. We've not really ever seen institutional transformation at this scale before. Not surprisingly it has taken a decade to get from vision to stable reality."

Oracle bounced back nicely from that long-delayed Fusion project and today it has the widest set of cloud SKUs—software, platform, infrastructure, data-as-a-service offerings, etc. As Thomas Kurian, President of Product Development at Oracle, told *Fortune*, "Now, on average on a daily basis, 62 million people log in and use our cloud for various things."[68]

Teter added:

"Fusion has come such a long way. The move from on-premise to SaaS masks the technical footprint complexity to customers, and Oracle has a compelling story of agility for rapidly changing markets. The Oracle sales teams are much better trained and indeed incented to sell Cloud solutions first."

and

"They still have work to do, of course. There's still confusion in product lines and offerings—what's Fusion, what's SaaS, etc. The UX is still not homogenous across

---

[68] http://fortune.com/2015/06/08/redemption-of-mark-hurd-oracle/

modules. Much of services-based integration is SOAP-based and slow; customers would like a much quicker move to REST standards."

The Fusion delay highlights a phenomenon common in enterprise software—next-gen products take much longer to deliver than is anticipated by most vendors. It also highlights that often, while the initial next-gen project may seem like a waste, the experience leads to innovation in unexpected places. One such example comes from Oracle HCM products.

Oracle has launched a series of work/life apps, one of which is focused on reputation management. This app provides a clearer picture of how a candidate or employee is viewed by peers and the communities he/she works across, thereby enhancing the social glimpses LinkedIn and other networks provide. Another app focuses on wellness and competition with peers, using growing "quantified self" data that Fitbit, Apple Watch and other personal wearable technologies are generating. More apps are coming in the work/life category, including one on "my career development" which allows employees to benchmark themselves against career paths and even evaluate their fit for roles in other parts of their enterprises.

Sumser noted:

"The profile/reputation toolset is astonishing in its ambition. It seems like Oracle is tackling that question with an eye on scale. A rigorous and secure version of the tool is how people can operate in a world where ties between employees and employers are weaker. There is no one who sees the questions more clearly."

Another new area is the Oracle Learning Cloud which sources content from both internal and external sources, including YouTube and massive open online courses (MOOCs), and personalizes recommendations for training paths. Here you can catch glimpses of how Oracle is using its global network of cloud data centers and technology talent to support transcoding and bit-rate-adaptive video streams. These are designed to remove latency issues as users publish and consume content on a wide range of networks—slow 3G cellular or speedier WiFi-supported bandwidth.

Sumser added:

> "The new learning platform makes enterprise organizations able to harvest social media for learning purposes. This is infrastructure that encourages the grass roots development of learning. That's what agile companies do."

The JD Edwards OneWorld Experience

A much more sobering next-gen story comes from the JD Edwards experience as it migrated its ERP solution from the proprietary IBM AS/400 platform to the open, client/server world.

Through the 1990s, Michael Schmitt held several senior positions at JD Edwards, including GM, Central Europe, and SVP of Sales and Marketing. He described to me the next-gen product experience at JD Edwards:

> "By the mid-nineties, JD Edwards had become the leader in the AS/400 ERP marketplace. With the market demanding client/server solutions, most AS/400 vendors had

embarked on rewrites from RPGIII on the AS/400 to C+/ C++ applications on UNIX and other open hardware.

JD Edwards, with a project that had started in the early 90s, delivered its open version called OneWorld in 1996. It was timely, and with our going IPO in 1997, was meant to help deliver to the higher top line expectations of a public software company.

In many ways, OneWorld was quite an accomplishment, especially when you consider our competitors like Marcam, SSA (with BPCS), JBA and many other AS/400 vendors struggled or died trying to reach the land of open systems. OneWorld was designed with object-oriented principles and promised reusability of objects. The system was much more customer configurable and the development tools were more sophisticated. It had a much sexier user interface. It ran on OS/400, Unix and Windows NT hardware, and on multiple databases: AS/400, Oracle and SQL.

Looking back, however, we also made several mistakes with OneWorld. The software tried to emulate the AS/400 version of World Software and match its data schema. Many of the developers came from the AS/400 RPG world, versus C+. We were resource constrained when we should have been working on new functionality for emerging markets like CRM, supply chain planning and eProcurement. OneWorld gave little benefit to existing World Software customers whose maintenance fees paid for the development.

The new system was riddled with bugs and scalability issues and our developers were caught in a cycle of patches and fixes. The software was highly complex and difficult to install, so our engineers were brought into early customer implementations putting stress on constrained resources with knowledge of the new technology. Being public at this stage, the company was driven to deliver topline revenue results. That may have come at the expense of product maturity and the customer experience.

Looking back, customers who waited for the software to reach stability and for critical mass of support personnel to implement the software did much better. In my estimation, stability and critical mass occurred sometime after five years from original launch.

PeopleSoft acquired JD Edwards in 2003. It was the end of a very proud run for our Colorado culture. Our destiny was hugely influenced by the years it took us to develop and mature OneWorld."

Let's next look at an even more ambitious project at Microsoft.

Microsoft's "Project Green"

In 2000, Microsoft acquired Great Plains, which was then a leading mid-market ERP vendor, though primarily in the U.S. In 2002, it acquired Navision, which was a leading ERP vendor in Europe. Each of these companies had made their own acquisitions, and Microsoft found itself with four ERP products—Great Plains, Navision, Axapta and Solomon.

In 2003, Microsoft began working on an effort code named Project NextGen, which later morphed into Project Green.

Frank Scavo, President of Strativa, a California-based management consulting firm that helps companies evaluate software alternatives, commented in an interview:

> "None of these acquired products had been written purely with the Microsoft technology stack. Axapta, for example, had been written in its own development environment (MorphX), in its own language (X++), using Oracle as its preferred database. Project Green was aimed at converting the four products to Microsoft technology and unifying to a single code base while retaining the best features of each product."

Four years later, Mary Jo Foley, one of the best-known Microsoft media followers, summarized:

> "Microsoft must rue the day a few years back that the company hatched the 'Project Green' idea."[69]

The project was far more complex than Microsoft had anticipated, and in 2005, Doug Burgum, then Microsoft Senior Vice President, acknowledged:

> "It's a tough challenge . . . . Some of it was expected to be tough, and some of it was even tougher than what was expected."[70]

Scavo provided color commentary:

---

[69] http://www.zdnet.com/article/microsofts-project-green-still-alive-and-kicking/
[70] http://www.zdnet.com/article/microsoft-slow-going-in-biz-software-push/

"In 2004, I knew they had reduced the number of developers assigned to Project Green from 200 to about 70. Then in 2005, Microsoft began to talk about rollout waves. The first wave, slated from 2005 through 2007, would incorporate into the products' common Microsoft technologies, such as Microsoft's Sharepoint portal, its workflow engine and SQL Server business intelligence capabilities. This wave would also create a common Web services architecture among the products to facilitate integration. The second wave, through 2009, would allow the products to take advantage of features in Microsoft's next generation Longhorn operating system and the next version of its Visual Studio developer tools. And there was the distant possibility of a third phase—the merge of the four products into a single code base."

Beyond the project complexity, there were the market realities.

More from Scavo :

"Microsoft found that most customers were not eager to face a major upgrade/migration to a new product. Worse, competitors used Project Green as a scare tactic since what Microsoft was selling short-term was going to be replaced by a new product."

What the project did deliver was some similarity in look and feel and common reporting capabilities across products.

"We think that over time we will add technology to the products that will be similar, like the SharePoint integration, like Web services, like the UI . . . It doesn't make them one code base, but it does make them closer to one another," said Mogens Munkholm Elsberg, then responsible for Microsoft strategy around the Dynamics products.

Microsoft also rebranded all its ERP products as Dynamics. Axapta became Dynamics AX; Great Plains, Dynamics GP; Navision, Dynamics NAV; and Solomon, Dynamics SL."

Scavo commented:

> "I never thought converging the four products was a realistic objective. When Microsoft finally gave up Project Green in 2007, I said that it would remove the uncertainty about the future of those products. They were good products at the time, and since then, with renewed development by Microsoft, they have gotten even better. Dynamics AX is now a credible alternative to SAP and Oracle in many global deals, and Dynamics NAV is a widely implemented solution for the small and midsize business market worldwide. Both products are now available on Microsoft Azure. I think Microsoft has been far better off developing these products independently in response to market needs than it would have been making a huge and risky technical migration to a common code base."

Next, let's look at the industry's most recent next-gen enterprise software effort.

Infor's CloudSuite Project

In March 2015, C-level executives from a wide range of sectors, including hospitality, local government, healthcare and contract manufacturing, attended a gathering in New York. Four years ago, they would have had little in common to talk about from a business perspective, but during this session they were animated about user experiences and cloud data centers.

The meeting was another milestone in an ambitious make-over in progress at Infor, the New York City-based software vendor. The company had once been called an "ERP grave-yard," as Infor had accumulated a wide portfolio of ERP brands including Baan, Lawson, MAPICS, SSA Global Technologies and Systems Union. Those in turn had made acquisitions of their own (such as Lawson buying Intentia). Since they arrived in late 2010, Infor CEO Charles Phillips and his team have been rein-vigorating the company which Phillips has called the "world's largest start-up." Infor has over 70,000 customers and over $2.5 billion in revenue and Phillips has invested in rationalizing and modernizing the inherited portfolio.

To start with, Infor has chosen to focus on 15 vertical CloudSuite modules (such as automotive, fashion, and food and beverage) and three horizontal ones (including corporate and human capital management).

I interviewed Cindy Jutras, President of the ERP analyst firm Mint Jutras. She commented:

> "Adding specialized functionality for all these verticals to a single, general-purpose ERP solution would add an unwanted level of complexity for every customer. On the other hand, maintaining many different solu-tions that share some common requirements is a waste of development resources for the ERP vendor. So Infor has identified from its portfolio a handful of solutions. In the case of food and beverage, for example, M3 is the

selected ERP solution. Infor then builds out the requirements for dairy or beer or processed meats as optional add-on components."

Infor next invested in "glue" across these offerings via its ION middleware. The fundamental building block here is the Business Object Document (BOD) schema for common business transaction types in OAGIS, the XML-based interface which has been evolving over the last 20 years. This has allowed Infor to simplify integration among its portfolio of applications. It also allows customers to extend messages with industry-specific overlays without breaking the basic BOD format. These messages get collected in a "Business Vault" available for access by analytical tools, or via workflow and alerts to be shared across a wide range of interfacing systems and by mobile and social access.

Jutras continued:

"All of Infor's strategic product lines have been "IONized." This means Infor can develop functionality that can be shared across many of its different products, including horizontal solutions such as customer relationship management (CRM), human capital management (HCM), supplier exchanges and more, as well as localizations that deal with local country requirements in transacting basic business."

Next there was a beautification project to redefine the software user experience. Different from other software vendors, Infor's UX has not been defined by developers, but instead was created using a captive, in-house design agency, Hook & Loop. The agency has over one hundred creative staff with credentials such as a Pulitzer Prize winner for infographics, the digital effects editor of the movie *The Avenger* and a fashion designer for Kenneth Cole.

As Jutras explained:

> "This team isn't developing the software. It is just designing what it will look like and how the users will interact with it. As a result it is unfettered by all the distractions of the programming that very often leads developers down rat holes, creating added complexity."

In a departure from other software vendors, Infor has chosen to use its data center infrastructure from Amazon Web Services. Infor's Co-President Duncan Angove explained in an interview:

> ". . . It's a scale game. Amazon has got 5 times more storage and compute capacity than the next fourteen guys combined. . . . It's like comparing someone that builds jumbo jets to someone that tries to do it on their own as a hobby. . . . And by the way, because we are not having to make those (data center) investments, we are able to invest in the application tier."[71]

Infor has also been able to leverage a recent industry trend towards analytical applications and machine learning, with the

---

[71] http://diginomica.com/2014/11/12/infor-hits-back-criticism-decision-use-aws-cloudsuite/

creation of its Dynamic Science Labs. Based in Cambridge, MA, the unit is recruiting talent from leading local schools like MIT.

Another initiative aimed more at upgrading/migrating customers is Infor's UpgradeX program. It is designed to cluster legacy product customers toward a modernized CloudSuite. So, the path for those running older versions of Baan, LN, XA, XPPS and Trans4M customers is called LN, and customers are most likely to be guided toward CloudSuite modules aimed at aerospace and defense, auto or industrials. Those running M3 (formerly Intentia's Movex), LX, Adage and System2l are likely steered to the M3 path aimed toward food and beverage, fashion or equipment sector modules.

The UpgradeX package is a series of tools supplemented by consulting and education services. One of the more interesting features of this package is the value engineering work performed by a team of Infor (and partner) specialists. The leadership of this group came from SAP which had done similar studies for its customers in previous years. At Infor, they have significantly expanded their database of benchmarks and value drivers. They have also developed value apps for each of the industry groups that Infor services and they have updated TCO models using more recent cloud metrics. As of April 2015, they claimed to showcase 300 value engineering projects with customers. Infor is also making UpgradeX financially attractive by allowing existing customers to trade their existing maintenance fees for subscription fees to the new systems.

Scavo, introduced above, likes the UpgradeX package, but has expressed concern in a post about whether the implementation ecosystem can scale:

"It's a tall order. When new enterprise software vendors go to market (e.g., NetSuite, FinancialForce, Kenandy, Rootstock and other cloud-only providers), their installed base counts are relatively small. Even if they grow rapidly, the number of experienced implementation consultants grows in relationship to the growth in the installed base. Each go-live is an opportunity for more professionals to receive training in the new system.

But in the case of Infor, it acquired 70,000 customers— an enormous number—over a relatively short period. Furthermore, these customers are running a wide variety of Infor systems, some of which can truly be considered legacy systems. When Infor sells an UpgradeX deal, it needs implementation resources who not only know the target systems, but also the legacy systems."[72]

So, in many ways, Infor has made many pioneering and smart investments over the last five years. However, even after this sizable investment, the next-gen product and the legacy customer base migration is a work-in-progress.

As we have seen earlier with Oracle, Microsoft and JD Edwards, a next-gen product takes years of development and maturation. Migrating a legacy customer base takes even longer.

Those are just the laws of physics. SAP may be able to bend these laws slightly with S/4, but will likely not be able to break them.

SAP NetWeaver and BYD Initiatives
SAP's attempts at next-gen products have had their own challenges. In 2003, with fanfare, SAP introduced NetWeaver.

---

[72] http://strativa.com/infor-erp-customers-and-the-upgradex-roadmap/

TechTarget wrote back then:

> "When SAP executive board member Shai Agassi talks about NetWeaver, he speaks of miracles, Red Seas parting and a new belief system. The company's new technology stack, Agassi says, offers salvation for anyone buried under the costs and complexities of integration products. Embarking on a 50-city tour in 2004, SAP is preparing to show off the company's newly packaged integration platform."[73]

Network World wrote:

> "Based on Web services and aimed at easing users' integration headaches, NetWeaver can link disparate applications and data sources, allowing companies to make use of their existing IT investments and personnel skills while exploiting the power of Web services, SAP says."[74]

The NetWeaver scope grew over the years and a market analyst described the evolution:

> "Many outside analysts viewed NetWeaver as a middleware integration play, which it was, but it was also an umbrella for many SAP tools and solutions. As an integration play it largely failed to live up to its fanfare, though the Process Integration (PI) component, while

---

[73] http://searchsap.techtarget.com/news/956297/Shai-Agassis-passion-NetWeaver
[74] http://www.networkworld.com/article/2339735/software/sap-unveils-netweaver-middleware.html

heavy handed and not good with lightweight web/SaaS integration, has pretty good penetration in large SAP shops that are mostly SAP centric."

Customer adoption was slow and with Agassi leaving in 2007, SAP's passion for NetWeaver started to cool. I asked the CEO of a Business Process Management (BPM) vendor his recollection of NetWeaver in the field and he responded, "I think it was a total flop. Remember it was trying to sell to a platform market which SAP's application focused field was not familiar with."

Outwardly, SAP persisted with NetWeaver, and a SAP press release in 2010 read:

> "The current quarter has seen 200 new customers embrace SAP NetWeaver PI, and adoption of SAP NetWeaver PI has grown nearly tenfold since the first half of 2006."[75]

In the meantime, the market perception was that the technology was already being phased out:

> "Still, Tuesday's announcement was a strong show of support for NetWeaver, which some observers believe has suffered from a lack of development in comparison to competing stacks from Oracle and IBM. That perception has helped fuel rumors that SAP will at some point purchase a major middleware vendor such as Tibco or Software AG."[76]

---

[75] http://www.prnewswire.com/news-releases/new-release-of-sap-netweaver-paves-the-way-for-future-innovation-104756604.html
[76] http://www.pcworld.com/article/207512/saps_netweaver_isnt_dead_yet.html

An analyst recently summarized the limited state of NetWeaver today:

> "Today, the real lasting remnant of NetWeaver, is Solution Manager. SolMan has some adoption in big SAP shops but is really a heavy set of system management tools that work only for SAP shops willing to invest in a complex tool kit, and are a hindrance, a curse, or an afterthought in most others."

The path of SAP's Business ByDesign (BYD) was even more winding. The following are excerpts from a post by Dennis Howlett of Diginomica in July 2014:

> "Sometime in the 2003–4 timeframe, Zencke (then head of SAP R&D) proposed a new suite aimed at SMBs that could be run as a hosted solution. At the time, cloud as we now know it was very much in its infancy. In essence, Zencke reckoned you could take core parts of the SAP R/3 process engine and wrapper them with web services to create . . . voila!—a cloud offering that would complement and enhance the overall product portfolio.
>
> Unfortunately, by the time SAP was ready to hit the market sometime around 2007–8, and had spent many millions in developing ByDesign, the world had moved on. At the initial launch, there was quiet if skeptical approval.
>
> At its architectural core, ByDesign was not built as a multi-tenant solution and SAP quickly discovered that scaling out was a costly nightmare for a solution that

could never turn a profit . . . At that stage, SAP withdrew it from the market and spent 18 months re-engineering so that it could get better operational metrics and performance. It was still a mini R/3 with an interface to match although not as crappy as many in use at the time.

Quarters came and went, SAP talked up the BYD numbers, eventually plateauing at something like 1,000 customers. Of those, roughly 250 were what you'd call 'friends and family' so that the real in market sales were a paltry 700–750 and stagnating.

In 2012 along came Lars Dalgaard via the SuccessFactors acquisition and what did he do? He blew up the ByDesign suite into pieces, saying that people wanted to buy functionality and not the suite. I was flabbergasted. In all the years I've been around software, I've never seen or heard such an insane idea. SAP did nothing to stop him, in the belief that as the only guy at board level with cloud experience, he must know best.

Some people got it and efforts were made to bring that vision to market along with some nice UI touches that added sparkle to BYD. But SAP's core development was firmly focused on HANA and within 20 months, SAP had pretty much canned BYD development. That is pretty much where we are today, other than some re-engineering to put BYD onto HANA and the maintenance of existing customers."[77]

---

[77] http://diginomica.com/2014/07/18/deconstructing-saps-smb-strategy-and-bydesign/#.VEjGbof7ifs

Howlett posted a reversal a few months later:

> "It turns out that commentary was only partially correct because of some misdirection by SAP but also because we were not fully aware of what was going on internally. SAP chose not to disavow me or others of our opinion and BYD promptly fell off all RFP lists."[78]

While Howlett described BYD as "alive and kicking" in his revision, it's taken a decade and still does not account for even one percent of SAP's customers or its revenues.

S/4HANA—The Sum of All Industry Experiences?

The common thread across all the next-gen projects described in this chapter is that in the enterprise world, new products take years to develop and then to mature. In the interim, vendors often meander or waver in their commitments. Customer bases, in turn, take decades to migrate.

SAP has a massive development army at its disposal, so the S/4 product creation process may be quicker. Still, the scope is daunting. In the Plattner/Leukert book, they describe the need to tackle 400 million lines of code in the SAP Business Suite.

TechVentive's Sommer wrote in 2013:

> "SAP users are using, by SAP's estimation, some 300,000 different input screens that were designed for different product lines, numerous product versions, different vertical industry requirements, etc. These screens were

---

[78] http://diginomica.com/2014/10/23/sap-business-bydesign-alive-kicking/

developed using approximately 20 different software tools."[79]

It is likely S/4 will tackle only a fraction of those screens that apply to Business Suite customers, but even that is a large project unto itself.

Then there is a cultural matter of even greater concern. In *SAP Nation* I had highlighted that the SAP development culture had gradually moved to one of a platform company with years of focus on NetWeaver, followed by HANA. S/4, like BYD, needs much more of an application culture.

There are plenty of questions about HANA as a transaction processing environment, and Fiori will need to keep evolving as users increasingly adjust to voice, gestural and other interfaces in their cars and homes. Functionality, long neglected in many verticals, will need to evolve to satisfy customer needs.

David Rowe, SVP and CMO at Rimini Street, which provides independent third party maintenance support to over 150 SAP customers, commented to me they are seeing increased interest from SAP customers since S/4 was announced:

> "If S/4HANA evolves into a proven and fully functional platform in the future, Independent Support clients can easily return and SAP will welcome them back with open arms given the nature of a highly competitive software landscape today. If S/4HANA follows the same pattern as BusinessByDesign, SAP CRM or SAP SRM, then the great news is that the customer has not pre-paid for failed

---

[79] http://www.zdnet.com/article/saps-ui-makeover-taking-a-measured-approach-to-300000-screens/

R&D, and instead has funded their own innovation that the business needs now, while maintaining the flexibility to choose the best proven option available in the market."

Let's next look at what impact the customer migration to S/4 may have on the GDP of the SAP economy.

CHAPTER 5

S/$HANA

↝

"It should be called S/$, not S/4. That's as "simple" as Shift4 on the keyboard."

Thus spoke an interviewee for this book, mocking SAP's relentless use of the word "simple" over the last year.

Actually, this person's focus on dollars is very appropriate. SAP's Enslin has projected "We will see at least 1,000 of the top 2,000 do some sort of (S/4) project in 2016. What's interesting is that we're seeing 41% as net new customers."[80] That means a crunch for talent familiar with the newer technologies, which often leads to premiums in the SAP consulting market even for more mature skills.

---

[80] http://diginomica.com/2015/07/21/saps-q2-fy2015-more-color-on-the-results-s4-is-acoming-hana-revived/?#.Va7JAvlVhBc

SAP promises its Activate "consumption experience"[81] embedded in S/4 should help streamline implementations. Previous SAP attempts with tools like Solution Manager, however, have not significantly improved performance in its ecosystem. Additionally, the "net new" customers are not likely to be as familiar with that poor track record in the SAP ecosystem and could end up with similarly significant over-runs and write-offs.

Outsourcers/Staffing Firm Costs

Elements of S/4 are already leading to an expansion of the SAP services ecosystem. Fiori has led to a cottage industry of consultants, such as Sodales Solutions in Toronto. Sana Salam, President of Sodales, notes:

> "Not too long ago, with the launch of SAP Fiori, we began to focus on the importance of simple design. Since the initial launch of Fiori in 2013 with 25 Fiori Apps, SAP Fiori app portfolio has grown to over 500 Fiori apps. Even though Fiori enables instant mobilization and simplification of business processes, standard out of the box apps only are not enough to address every business process, such as cross-platform business transactions or location-aware apps, etc. There is a huge need for designing custom apps that are context specific and can integrate with many platforms."[82]

---

[81] http://www.infotechlead.com/software/sap-unveils-sap-activate-allows-customer-to-deploy-sap-s4hana-32282
[82] http://scn.sap.com/community/best-built-applications/blog/2015/04/21/the-era-of-simple-design-why-you-should-build-custom-apps-on-hana-cloud-platform

The move to private clouds is opening up opportunities for a new generation of infrastructure providers like Virtustream. A harbinger of the size of S/4HANA projects: Just the infrastructure move to a private cloud can be a three- to-six month project.

There is a growing HANA talent pool, especially in SAP's Startup Focus program which claims 2,000 start-ups in 175 countries. They are focused on creating solutions like Feedzai on credit card fraud and NexVisionIX on retail store intelligence. For their own implementations, however, customers will likely rely on a new breed of HANA and other analytics-focused boutiques like Bluefin Solutions, Dolphin Solutions and itelligence AG.

Sommer of TechVentive (introduced in a previous chapter) painted a vivid picture of the likely complexity and labor intensity of S/4 as he walked along the partner booths at SAPPHIRE this year. He documented slogans at over 15 partners, all of which claimed to be "simple":

Grom—"Simplify Your Business"

HP—"Simplifying the Journey to Innovation"

WalkMe—"Instantly Simplify Your SAP Technology Environments"

LeverX—"Simplify Innovation & Engineering Excellence"

Revelation—"Simplify Change Control for SAP Solutions"

SGI—"Powerfully Simple"

Seal—"It is Simple! It is. Seal"

CSC—"Make it Simple"

IBM—"Simplify . . . with IBM"

EMC—"Simplify Your SAP Journey"

KNOA—"Simplify Migration With Knoa"

Capgemini—"Simplify with end-to-end solutions"

OpenText—"Simplify. Run Digital."

Fujitsu—"Inspiring Simplicity" and "Simplify Decision-Making With SAP Solutions"

Sommer's summary: "I was, **simply**, overwhelmed with the unanimity of scores of service firms all focused on simplicity."[83]

In reality, there is little that is simple about S/4 migration. It will call for implementation projects with elaborate change management, data conversion and testing requirements.

Customer Staff Costs

Bruce J. Rogow (about whom you'll hear more in Chapter 7), formerly of Gartner and now an adviser to many CIOs, pointed out in his review of *SAP Nation:*

> "Folks who have implemented or tried to implement an ERP tell me that the costs of internal business resources are equal to or more than the cost of outside or IT resources and software. *SAP Nation* doesn't include these costs."[84]

---

[83] http://diginomica.com/2015/05/14/selling-saps-run-simple-is-not-the-same-as-achieving-it/

[84] http://dealarchitect.typepad.com/deal_architect/2015/03/bruce-j-rogow-on-sap-nation.html

Other readers have made similar comments.

They are correct. While writing *SAP Nation,* I had constructed several models of the economy. One had included end-user costs and showed the GDP at over $400 billion a year (whereas the book used the model with $204 billion). When SAP brags on its Web site[85] that it has 80 million cloud subscribers and 130 million mobile users, even small allocations of cost per user can add up to hundreds of billions in dollars.

My thinking back then was, "What's the point of presenting an even gloomier model?"

But the new Fiori UX has a direct impact on end users. Working on a recent Fiori implementation, Petterøe (introduced in the previous chapter) commented, "We see that there isn't a need for training or retraining of end users at all! They intuitively understand the app." While that is encouraging, it would be reasonable to factor 20 hours a year of end user retraining impact, at a loaded cost of $75 an hour. So, even if you assume a fraction of SAP's claimed user counts—say, 30 million end users—you could be looking at an incremental cost of $45 billion a year.

The Revised GDP of SAP Nation

I adjusted the model I had presented in *SAP Nation* to project for the potential impact of Fiori, HANA and newer SAP acquisitions.

On the following page is the revised model:

---

[85] http://www.sap.com/bin/sapcom/en_us/downloadasset.2015-04-apr-21-01. SAP-Corporate-Fact-Sheet-en-20150421-pdf.bypassReg.html

SAP Economy Model
Estimates of annual SAP customer spending

Labor	Customers	Avg Staff	Headcount	Annual Unit Cost US $	Total US $ billions	Notes
Outsourcers/ Staffing firms						
Top 25			225,000	200,000	45	a
Next 100			75,000	180,000	14	b
Next 12,500			312,500	125,000	39	
Travel expenses					6	
Customer Staff						c
BusinessSuite	20,000	25	500,000	80,000	40	d
All-in-One	25,000	5	125,000	50,000	6	
BusinessOne	50,000	2	100,000	50,000	5	
Others	195,000	4	780,000	1,500	39	e
Endusers			30,000,000	1,500	45	f
Software						
SAP (incl Sap Service, and HEC)			75,000		20	g
Other - database, testing, BPM, training, integration					20	h
Infrastructure						
Hardware/hosting/ virtualization					20	i
Telecommunications					10	j
Totals	290,000				309	

a   Derived from multiple industry analyst estimates
b   From analysis of exhibitors at SAPPHIRE NOW with services offerings
c   SAP does not break out its customers by products. These are estimates from polling of various analysts
d   FTE of functional experts, Basis, ABAP/4, COE, program mgt, other SAP focused technical staff
e   Largely BusinessObjects, Ariba, SuccessFactors, Sybase customers.
f   Assumes 20 hours of retraining a year at $ 75 an hour
g   Includes SAP Services and Hana Enterprise Cloud
h   Spend on licenses, subscriptions, annual maintenance
i   Includes data centers, disaster recovery sites
j   Telecom equipment/MPLS circuits/carrier charges

Exhibit 1   Source: Deal Architect

The major adjustments are:

- As in previous upgrade cycles, there is often a shortage of qualified partner resources with customers having to pay premiums for such support. Often they end up using SAP's even more premium-priced consultants. I increased the annual cost of staff by $20,000 per head to reflect inflation common when there is new technology in the SAP economy. The average hourly rates at $90–100 are still conservative compared to what SAP itself and many of its partners charge customers.

- At its Global Partner Summit in June 2015, SAP shared that it had 13,000 partners worldwide. While many surely have a relatively small number of consulting staff (compared to a partner like Accenture), I have added an average of 25 staff for 12,500 of those partners I did not previously have in the model. SAP had provided feedback on the model but chose not to disclose I had underestimated that count.

- With the growing sprawl in the SAP product portfolio, I am seeing more customers invest in master data management, middleware and other internal projects with related staff. They are also having to invest in duplicate IT staff as they transition to HANA and Fiori while continuing to invest in existing technologies. I increased the staff count for the average Business Suite customer from 20 to 25.

- In the model in "SAP Nation," I did not have Concur customers as the acquisition had only recently closed. SAP is now reporting 291,000 customers, so I increased the staff count for "Others" (to include the most recent acquisitions) to 195,000.

- I added a new line for "end users," using the assumption above that 30 million users will each need 20 hours of training a year.

I could have added much larger end-user costs, growing costs of non-human users like smart meters, and amortization costs but let me repeat my guiding thought during *SAP Nation:* What's the point of presenting an even gloomier model? The revised model already puts the GDP of SAP Nation at over $300 billion a year—close to that of Israel.

"The Bastards Say, Welcome"

In the Pulitzer-prize-winning *The Soul of a New Machine,*[86] Tracy Kidder wrote of an ad that Data General produced but never ran. It read:

> "They Say IBM's Entry Into Minicomputers Will Legitimize The Market. The Bastards Say, Welcome"

Jason Blessing, the CEO of Plex, a cloud manufacturing vendor (and before that an executive at Taleo, a cloud HCM vendor), similarly told me:

> "Strange as it may sound, I am pleased to see S/4. First, SAP's cloud delivery promise and those of other major vendors like Oracle validates cloud computing and what we have been doing at Plex for years now. Second, any

---

[86] http://www.amazon.com/Soul-New-Machine-Tracy-Kidder/dp/0316491977/ref=sr_1_1?ie=UTF8&qid=1436230451&sr=8-1&keywords=The+Soul+Of+A+New+Machine

time a company announces a next-gen product it puts their incumbent customer base in play. Customers know they have to re-platform and therefore re-implement their old SAP applications. Any effort like that becomes an opportunity for Plex to show what we can do for customers in the cloud.

SAP may say S/4 is coming soon, but as we know, enterprise apps are complex. Look at Workday and Oracle Fusion. It's taken them a while to mature their cloud offerings. Additionally, SAP will need to adjust to our changed industry with the pay-as-you-go business model and more modular application sales. Our customers are poster children for those trends in the industry. They often start with a single plant and expand from there. Our private equity, cloud-savvy investors embraced the subscription model a long time ago. Our partners think small and sell based on their operational knowledge, not their big brands.

Being the last major software vendor to re-platform for the cloud, SAP does have the advantage of learning from the mistakes of others. On the other hand, being late puts more pressure on them, and likely they will only cosmetically refresh what they have today."

At an event in early 2015, the CIO of Stant, a new Plex customer, described its selection criteria for a new ERP solution. Having done the analysis on both the total cost and organizational burden of running an on-premise solution, she made cloud computing a primary requirement. Legacy ERP providers, including SAP, couldn't move forward in the selection process because they were unable to demonstrate cloud-based solutions.

Kustoff, introduced in the previous chapter, agrees:

> "This is the third major architectural shift I have seen in my IT career. Just like SAP capitalized on the move to client/server computing in the last wave, other vendors without a legacy and client base to support will pour in to take advantage of this shift."

Actually, many customers have taken to heart what I wrote in *SAP Nation*:

> "Such a large economy, as big as Ireland's, should have its own central bank, budget office, treasury, etc. The SAP economy is rudderless in comparison—there is no central management and few controls."

As the revised model shows, the economy is poised to get even more inflationary with the S/4 rollout. As a result, I expect many SAP customers to diversify their investments to what Gartner has called "postmodern ERP." In the next chapter, we will look at some of the customer coping strategies which may hold the economy in check from this projected inflation.

CHAPTER 6

Postmodern ERP

~~➤

Gartner has been talking about "postmodern ERP" for a couple of years now:

> "Businesses looking to improve administration today can take advantage of lower costs, better functional fit and process flexibility offered by blending cloud applications with on-premises applications in what we now refer to as 'postmodern ERP.'"[87]

While Gartner's definition mostly focuses on moves to cloud applications and business process outsourcing, in *SAP Nation* I described a wider range of customer coping strategies: two-tier, ring fencing, third-party maintenance, change in talent models, etc. The following chart summarizes the case studies I profiled and the proliferation of strategies.

---

[87] http://www.gartner.com/newsroom/id/2658415

Customer Strategies

Un-adopters	Diversifiers	Pragmatists	Committed
A1 – Flip it off	**B1** – "Ring Fence" with clouds	**C1** – Keep relationship analytical	**D1** – Align with SAPs Future
A2 – Freeze and Shrink	**B2** – Change Talent Model	**C2** – Keep projects low-hype	**D2** – Make SAP dance to your business tune
	B3 – Tiers of Joy	**C3** – Rethink the Customer Experience	
	B4 – Best of Breed for agility	**C4** – Balance with Open Source and commodity technology	

Exhibit 1   Source: Deal Architect

Feedback from several readers indicated they viewed the four customer categories as mutually exclusive. That was not what I intended. In actuality, customers are mixing and matching various strategies across the four customer types. Also, since *SAP Nation* was published, I have seen a veritable tsunami of other SAP customer examples using these strategies, with some unique adaptations.

In many ways, the situation reflects customers doing their own thing to "simplify" and optimize their SAP environments. Many customers started their initiatives before S/4HANA was announced, and with so many questions swirling around S/4, I expect others to join them in crafting their own coping strategies:

"Multiple Hubs"

Many airlines have designed networks where traffic moves along spokes connected to a hub at a central airport. The majors have multiple hubs around the world. Delta, as an example, has hubs at Atlanta's Hartsfield; Paris' Charles de Gaulle and other airports. Many SAP customers are moving to similar architectures with hubs for product engineering/R&D, customer facing, industry specific and back-office operations. SAP remains the hub for many back-office operations, with spokes coming from satellite applications we describe in the "ring fence" strategy below. More significantly, as they build a next-generation of smart products (with embedded sensors, software and other technology), many SAP customers are custom developing much of that product-centric hub. In some industries, even cross-licensing technology from competitors for some of the spokes is preferable to what they can buy from SAP. For *The Digital Enterprise*[88], a 2014 book by Karl-Heinz Streibich, CEO of Software AG, I had interviewed many SAP customers like Daimler, GE and Allianz. Hardly any of them mentioned SAP as they discussed their innovation strategies. Similarly, in the customer-facing hub, many customers are finding that Salesforce, Oracle and Adobe have made significant strides compared to SAP. The same is true for industry-specific processes. This is allowing customers to gradually shrink the role of the SAP hub in their overall IT investment strategy to that of limited back-office support.

"Ring Fence"

One common strategy among SAP customers is to "ring fence" back-office ERP functionality with specialist solutions. This approach gives them a chance to innovate at the edge and learn about newer cloud and other computing models. Examples

---

[88] http://www.amazon.com/Digital-Enterprise-Karl-Heinz-Streibich/dp/09897 56408/ref=sr_1_1?s=books&ie=UTF8&qid=1437947293&sr=1-1&keywords=the+ digital+enterprise

include HP, profiled in *SAP Nation*, which has ring fenced SAP with Salesforce, Workday and other SaaS tools.

HP also uses E2open for Order Promising and Response Planning, as well as deploying its Supply Chain Planning to sync components from suppliers with its contract manufacturers.

Around 50 of SAP's Business Suite users employ E2open's Cloud Connectivity to collaborate with trading partners. Avnet, the large distributor of electronic components (with 5 million-plus parts), replaced SAP's Global Available to Promise with E2open's E2PR for Order Promising and Response Planning. Avon, which sells four lipsticks every second and has been gradually implementing SAP, uses E2open applications for supply chain visibility and management of contract manufacturers. L'Oréal, another large cosmetics company, uses collaboration tools from E2open for supply planning, inventory and order management around SAP's modules. Shell, a large SAP customer, uses E2open to provide Supply Chain Visibility to track and trace materials that go into oil rigs.

Malher, a subsidiary of Nestlé (a large SAP customer) in South America, uses Infor's supply chain and other functionality. The Commonwealth of Pennsylvania and Kellogg, the cereal company, both use Infor's Enwisen for their HR shared services around an SAP ERP core. AkzoNobel, the global paint and coatings company, and ABB Power Technologies AB have a variety of Infor functionality surrounding SAP.

Unit4, which focuses on ERP for service industries, indicates that a wide range of its customers use their specific functionality around SAP implementations. ASML, Atos, Capgemini, HEMA and Nationale-Nederlanden are using Unit4's Absence Management suite to manage long-term absenteeism and ensure their people quickly reintegrate into their working environments.

H&M is using Unit4's Consolidation and Financial Performance Reporting product, Kongsberg Defence & Aerospace is using its Travel and Expense Management solution, and Folksam and Mölnlycke use its Cash Flow Planning product. BASF and Achmea use its Statutory Reporting module to manage their monthly, quarterly and annual close processes.

"Independent Support"

The analyst firm, Gartner reports[89] it is seeing a steady increase in inquiries about cancelling maintenance agreements with ERP vendors. This is certainly a popular strategy with many SAP customers, who are seeking third party maintenance from providers like Rimini Street. Such independent providers promise "a higher level of service, no required upgrades and annual support fee savings of 50 percent."

In "SAP Nation," I profiled Embraer, the Brazilian aerospace company, and United Biscuits, the UK snack company, and their experiences with Rimini.

Rimini says it now has over 150 SAP customers under contract, representing over $100 billion in customer revenues. Rowe, the CMO of Rimini introduced in the previous chapter, explained to me:

> "More and more SAP customers are now choosing Independent Support as a strategy to shift funds from expensive maintenance and unnecessary upgrades towards new innovation projects around the edges of their core SAP system. These customers are not waiting for a future S/4HANA product that may or may not deliver any value. They are investing in innovative cloud,

---

[89] http://info.riministreet.com/Gartner-What-to-Consider.html?src=ss&src=dt=rsi

mobility, social and big data solutions today while still keeping their options open for a future platform that will best suit their needs, S/4HANA or other options.

CIOs are winning awards for driving innovation with savings from Independent Support. This strategic flexibility to evolve and grow their SAP application landscape is very important to these leading CIOs as they recognize that they aren't frozen under Independent Support, nor do they need to be tethered to the vendor for 'hit or miss' innovation."

Newer customers of Rimini include Univar, a $10 billion global chemical distributor, where Rimini is supporting its SAP ECC version 5.0 and 6.0 environments. Erik Viens, Univar's CIO, has said the savings are allowing him to invest in developing CRM, business intelligence and eCommerce platforms and in transforming the company's customer experience.

Another customer is TT Electronics, a $1 billion UK-based electronics manufacturer, whose CIO Ed Heffernan has been quoted as saying "(SAP Maintenance) is effectively an added tax that I have to pay for with no value in return." TT blends Rimini support while using the savings to continue to buy new SAP licenses for its ECC 6.0 environment.

Incitec Pivot, a $3 billion Australian industrial chemical company that has been an SAP customer for over two decades, uses Rimini for its ECC 6.0 and BW support. Besides the savings, CIO Martin Janssen cites better service: "We receive very clear service levels and faster case resolution that we never had previously. Gives us the confidence we'll get things done. We have never had that confidence before."

Pedro Balista, CIO of Positivo Informática, a Brazilian technology company, is even more positive about Rimini support for his ECC 6.0 systems, citing the fact that the company already logged (and resolved) as many support tickets in two months with Rimini Street as it had in the last two years of SAP support.

It's true that most customers look at independent support for cost savings. However, many customers also find attractive the 30-minute guaranteed response for urgent issues, highly personalized service from what Rimini calls a Primary Support Engineer (PSE), support for customizations at no additional charge and the ability to run the existing SAP release with a promise of 15 years with no required upgrades.

"Two-Tier ERP"

In the 1980s, as AS/400s and LANs matured, many multinationals adopted two- or three-tier application strategies—a mainframe-based application for corporate, domestic subsidiaries and regional hubs, with decentralized versions, for international subsidiaries. JD Edwards (now part of Oracle), Platinum (now Epicor), Sage and other vendors were beneficiaries of such tiering strategies.

Things have evolved quite a bit since then. Now companies can go with SaaS systems for smaller subsidiaries, and as a result may not even need local IT support.

Many SAP customers have adopted two-tier strategies. NetSuite and Microsoft have particularly benefited as the solution for smaller subsidiaries.

As it expands across Southeast Asia, ASICS, which produces high-performance footwear, apparel and accessories, is implementing NetSuite while continuing to use SAP for corporate functions. The software division of HP is using one single unified instance of NetSuite OneWorld to run mission-critical business processes including order-to-cash, revenue recognition, multicurrency processing, intercompany transactions and multi-country taxation compliance.

Microsoft also boasts several two-tier successes. Hunter Douglas, the home furnishings company, has been running Dynamics AX in its European operations and is now rolling it out across most of its manufacturing and fulfillment sites in South America. Invatec, a medical devices sub of Medtronic, has implemented Dynamics at several of its design and distribution locations in the U.S. and Europe.

Unit4 reports that many Caterpillar dealers rely on its financial software to fulfill complex reporting needs for corporate office as well as in-house needs (in a variety of currencies), and for integration with other operational systems including Caterpillar product databases. Unit4 Financials provides visibility into market trends with its new and used sales, rentals, services and replacement parts, as well as cross-industry solutions for mining, heavy construction, compact construction, energy exploration and agriculture.

SAP's own products, Business One and Business ByDesign, also target two-tier opportunities similar to the ones described above, and often work out to be more economical and flexible than Business Suite in secondary locations.

"Rip and Replace"

While this is an extreme move, many midsized companies, especially those being spun off or being taken over by private equity investors, often look at that "life event" as an opportunity to replace SAP products. In *SAP Nation*, for example, I had described Inteva's move to Plex upon its spinoff from Delphi, the large auto component supplier.

At a Microsoft meeting last fall, I heard an executive from Kodak Alaris, a spinoff from Eastman Kodak Co., a long-time SAP customer, describe its decision to go with Microsoft Dynamics and its Azure cloud. There are several other Microsoft customers who have replaced SAP, including Comptel, the Finnish telecom vendor; Piaggio Aerospace, the aerospace company based in Italy; and Sapa Group, the Norwegian maker of extruded aluminum profiles. Dentsply, the dental equipment company, has been standardizing on Microsoft, moving away from SAP, Oracle and Infor at several locations. Other than Comptel, the others are all multibillion-dollar entities in SAP's sweet spot.

Still other SAP customers are switching to NetSuite products. Commco LLC, a distribution and light manufacturing company, RedBuilt, a commercial construction contractor, and Penguin Computing swapped out Business Suite. Brother Max, which focuses on care and feeding products for babies and toddlers, replaced SAP's BusinessOne with NetSuite. Adminovate, an enterprise software and consulting provider in the life, health and annuities industries, replaced SAP Business ByDesign with NetSuite.

In *SAP Nation*, I had profiled how Middlesbrough Council in the UK was replacing SAP with Unit4. Unit4 has since told me about similar moves at U.S.-based Travel Leaders Group, a $20 billion travel management company, the German government entity Staatsbetrieb Sächsisches Immobilien- und Baumanagement and Netherlands-based CGIAR, an international consortium of nonprofit agricultural research organizations.

"Next-Gen Application Management"

One of the largest cost components in the SAP economy is application management, much of it outsourced. That segment is being challenged to automate its labor, and also transition away from the traditional headcount-based business model to one as-a-service.

Frank Casale, a long-time observer of the outsourcing industry, has projected:

> "Making the pivot to Robotic Process Automation (RPA) is a decisive moment for service providers. The benefits of digital labor are rapidly eclipsing the benefits of physical labor, and service providers can choose or decline to translate that into success. I forecast that by 2020, as much as 40 percent of information technology outsourcing (ITO) and business process outsourcing (BPO) service providers will be out of business or acquired by larger enterprises, if they fail to embrace the change and reinvent their business models."[90]

Phil Fersht, founder of HfS, an outsourcing-focused analyst firm, has been forecasting the emergence of the "as-a-service economy," and wrote this past May:

> "What struck me was how quickly our industry has genuinely become focused on achieving business outcomes over the past few months, and this is being woven into many of today's new contracts and governance performance metrics. The conversation has moved along

---

[90] http://www.irpanetwork.com/ebook-primer/

quite markedly and I view this is a major leap forward for many industry stakeholders to change the way we manage service delivery that isn't purely based on valueless metrics and squeezing out those last remnants of bloated labor cost."[91]

Former SAP CTO, Vishal Sikka, now heads Infosys, a major SAP implementer and application management firm. Infosys announced a significant commitment to automation. "The company has set a long-term internal target of up to 70% automation in its infrastructure management business, and up to 55% automation in its business process outsourcing business. Currently, 35–40% of its BPO processes are automated."[92]

One of the automation moves at Infosys has been acquisition of Panaya, the tool vendor described earlier in the book.

There are other potential savings from swapping application management providers. The Indian outsourcer HCL calls it "rebid" business and "guarantees" over 30 percent cost reduction using its proprietary ALT ASM framework. It has done well replacing incumbents like Accenture, Deloitte, HP and other Indian providers in many SAP outsourcing deals.

The following comes from some of the anonymized case studies HCL has shared:

For a CPG company: "HCL's ability to not only come in and take on operations, but also add incremental value in terms of ensuring portfolio wide visibility and enabling a business-aligned IT organization, but creating a model wherein this

---

[91] http://www.horsesforsources.com/#sthash.no1CpRJk.dpuf
[92] http://articles.economictimes.indiatimes.com/2015-05-12/news/62082970_1_infosys-ceo-vishal-sikka-automation-business-process

customer could move towards business process KPI monitoring, rather than just the traditional incident management."

For a high-tech company: "HCL is responsible for all SAP build and configuration activities (for manufacturing, CRM, Pricing, Product and Solution Configuration, Sales & Operational Planning) with additional support given for technical solution architecture. In addition, HCL also provides all integration development work using a custom-built solution developed jointly with the client."

For a beverage company: "Today after several years, both client and HCL are able to manage and monitor key process KPIs like Out of Stock and On Time in Full, rather than tracking traditional SLA metrics like Response Time, Resolution Time, etc."

"Next-Gen Infrastructure"

A number of SAP customers have been changing hosting providers and moving to private clouds from providers including Virtustream, itelligence and Secure-24. As we discussed in Chapter 1, private clouds provide only a fraction of the economic benefits of public clouds, but many customers would prefer not to give up their customizations or feeling of control, and private clouds give them a level of virtualization savings compared to their prior hosting contracts.

Virtustream (recently acquired by EMC) reports over 125 SAP customers, including Florida Crystal, the large manufacturer of sweetener products. Virtustream describes the improvement at this 20-plus TB customer:

> "Previously, an entire month-end workload typically took three days to run. FCC was able to run the same workload

in roughly four hours on ECC "Powered by HANA" in the Virtustream HANA Cloud farm. In addition, running in Virtustream's Enterprise Class Cloud, SAP HANA's response time improved by 50–500% across many of the core SAP business transactions and reports."[93]

Velocity Technology Solutions specializes in private clouds across SAP, Oracle, Infor and other ERP environments. It also provides more than just hosting services. For example, in its arrangement with BCBG, a fashion house, Velocity took over support for its JD Edwards, SAP, ACS and PkMS systems for its financials, retail management, apparel management and warehouse management, respectively. They were migrated from on-premise data centers and other hosting providers to Velocity's Virtual Private Cloud and covered by Velocity's Managed Application Services & Managed Disaster Recovery.

For HA International (HAI), a leading manufacturer of specialty chemicals, Velocity provided SAP implementation, hosting and managed services. It also supports a global helpdesk.

HCL, described above, also claims the ability to perform better than the competition in SAP infrastructure contracts. At a client where it replaced a large infrastructure outsourcer, it cites, "The client, after a seven-year contract with the incumbent, decided to move away to bring about innovation, in IT. The existing model was not cost efficient and didn't allow the customer to move to the cloud effectively. HCL's ability to not only bring about innovation but also enable this customer to bring about efficient operations based on process and SIAM

---

[93] https://www.constellationr.com/content/sna2013/don-whittington-florida-crystals-corporation

(service integration and management) helped this customer to manage other suppliers effectively."

Additionally, as competitors like Infor and Unit4 use Amazon and Microsoft infrastructure-as-a-service, many SAP customers are also experimenting with public cloud infrastructures on their own. Finally, incumbent SAP hosting providers are also offering newer choices. Examples include IBM with its SoftLayer cloud acquisition and HP with its CloudSystem services.

"Play Small Ball"

Petterøe, the EVRY consultant introduced earlier, provides a glimpse of smaller projects that customers are undertaking with newer SAP technologies. She says, "We developed a travel and expense application using standard SAP finance and HR functionality. SAP delivers templates as a way to get up and running with Fiori fast. So mostly it is the SAP standard app which is implemented and then extended to fit the customer's needs.

"As I see it, replacing all screens with Fiori front-ends for Business Suite on HANA would take too long and would involve too much work, so if you want an end-to-end Fiori experience for your Business Suite, S/4HANA is the way to go. But for many clients, just focusing on Fiori apps where that makes sense will likely be the better path."

Several customers have also been taking advantage of SAP's growing portfolio of Rapid Deployment Solutions (RDS). Gene Cao of Forrester reports that "The RDS concept aims to provide everything out of one box; clients buy a bundle of application and implementation services. RDS services have brought tangible benefits to clients that want to quickly start their SAP journey or begin with pilot implementations before going for a full-scale rollout."

However, Cao cautions, "Fast-growing businesses in dynamic economies like China's need to change their business processes often to sustain growth. Although SAP based RDS processes on best practices, every client has its own unique processes. If a customer implements fixed-scope RDS services and they don't meet expectations, the customer will have to submit a lot of change requests—which may lead to frustration and end in disappointment."[94]

SAP also continues to evolve its ASAP rapid implementation methodology, now in its eighth iteration.

As I wrote in *SAP Nation*, "ASAP (AcceleratedSAP) was a methodology launched in 1997 after SAP had started selling R/3 years prior. It was a defensive response to growing complaints that SAP implementations were too complex. So, ASAP focused on basic SAP-centric tasks such as configuration of tables. Its systems integration partners rightly complained that tasks such as data conversion, integration with legacy systems and organizational change management were given short shrift in ASAP."

ASAP continues to be focused on core SAP functionality. Given all the sprawl in SAP Nation, customers need to be aware of that limitation, but thinking small with SAP projects is healthy given the track record of project failures in that economy.

"Leverage SAP's Cannibalization"

SAP itself has shown a willingness to trade or partially retire existing licenses, "when consuming new innovations from SAP." That typically means new HANA licenses or multiyear

---

[94] http://blogs.forrester.com/gene_cao/13-11-25-use_caution_when_considering_rds_services_for_sap_implementations

subscription contracts on its Ariba, SuccessFactors and other cloud products.

Clearly, SAP is eager to report larger cloud revenues to Wall Street, so taking advantage of that eagerness may work for some customers. Customers report, however, that even in competitive deals, SAP's cloud pricing is aspirational. It reflects a premium which has long disappeared in the enterprise software market. Or they talk from both sides of the mouth, alternatively defending their on-premise software and then claiming to be a cloud company.

Other customers report "gun to the head" behavior. In a spin-off situation, SAP demanded a hefty assignment fee, but offered an alternate multiyear contract on its cloud products, which the customer did not need. In another such situation, SAP threatened to invoke its "indirect access" clause (a tactic many customers report)—again, the customer was offered a cloud subscription as an alternative.

For some customers, an early opportunity around procuring services may come from SAP's One Service which it piloted in China and is rolling out globally. ZDNet said, "In a nutshell, SAP's ONE Service will put its services in one unit. Services will now have one revenue line in future results and include premium and professional services. It's worth noting that the bulk of SAP deployments are delivered by outside consulting firms."[95]

Anecdotal evidence from early adopters in Asia suggests that ONE, at least in its early stages, is not making things "simple."

---

[95] http://www.zdnet.com/article/sap-cuts-2017-outlook-sees-cloud-profit-power-in-2020/

Some of its teething problems I heard about from customers:

> "Major challenge with SAP is that they cannot identify
> the right resources. This has not improved with One. As
> an example, SAP searched for 2 months to find a skilled
> resource on SAP Personas/NetWeaver Business Client,
> but has yet to find anyone. We turned to their own net-
> works to identify people in the market."

And:

> "We spent four weeks with SAP to identify an SRM
> specialist to perform a QA. After spending two weeks
> understanding the background, that resource was pulled
> onto another project with a secondary person needing
> to take over. We were under the impression that with
> One we would get better resource booking/priority but
> this has not been the case."

The sample of customers diversifying their SAP investments I have presented above is actually pretty small. Oracle,
Salesforce and several point-solution vendors could name many
additional customer examples.

Some SAP purists shake their heads at many of these strategies, especially those that cause customers to drift away from
the integrated ERP core. However, that core is a mirage today
given all the acquisitions SAP has made in the last decade which
it still has not fully integrated.

Andy Kyte, Gartner fellow, has an even better justification
for diversification:

> "When ERP was in its heyday, CEOs and business execu-
> tives wanted reliable and integrated solutions, so they

seized upon ERP as the way to provide this . . . Business stakeholders still want these same qualities, but now they assume that these qualities will be present in any software solution, and their requirements have switched to the twin concerns of lowering IT costs and seeking increased flexibility. A system that is not sufficiently flexible to meet changing business demands is an anchor, not a sail, holding the business back, not driving it forward."[96]

Kyte's comment is about ERP system flexibility. In many ways, as we show in the next chapter, SAP customers are finding the people supporting the system also need to be more flexible.

---

[96] http://www.gartner.com/newsroom/id/2658415

CHAPTER 7

Make the Problem Bigger

∿➤

Bill Joy is a legend in the IT industry with his contributions to the UNIX operating system, the Java language and the Sun SPARC processor, earning him the moniker, "Edison of the Internet" from *Fortune* magazine.

A decade ago, he took on something very different from his IT focus when he helped the venture capital firm Kleiner, Perkins, Caufield and Byers evaluate a wide portfolio of clean-tech investments.

In *The New Polymath*, I cited him saying:

> "If you cannot solve the problem, make the problem bigger. If you draw a bigger circle, you start to see several systems you can work on."

Joy needed to cast a wide net to enable Kleiner Perkins to evaluate nearly 5,000 investment opportunities around the world. A very big "circle" was needed to cover the science around solar energy, carbon sequestration, fuel cells, insulation, electric cars and many additional areas of sustainability and green technologies.

The SAP "Circle"

I read *"The In-Memory Revolution: How SAP HANA Enables Business of the Future,"* the new book written by Dr. Plattner and Leukert, to get a sense for the planning behind S/4HANA. On the surface, the "circle" they drew when they started planning in March 2012 (their timing according to the book) sounds daunting. They had to rewrite 400 million lines of code in the Business Suite, optimize it for HANA and Fiori and also make it deployable in the cloud. And as they say on several occasions, they were also challenged to make it "nondisruptive to customers." In 2012, SAP reported it had 183,000 customers in 24 countries, so making it nondisruptive to such a wide audience was intimidating.

In some ways, however, they began with too *small* a "circle." The initial scope for S/4 did not include their industry solutions or any of their Business One, BYD, BusinessObjects or other products SAP already had in its portfolio.

Then they have kept on digging a bigger hole for themselves. In 2012, they had barely consummated the SuccessFactors acquisition, and since then they have acquired Ariba, Concur, hybris, Fieldglass and many other companies. SAP also keeps chasing after new industries—especially sexier ones like sports teams—thus adding to its development backlog. Its product teams had to catch up to waves of new mobile, social and other technologies. To show off those investments, SAP claims volumes of 130 million mobile users and 18 million Jam users. All these users will need migrations, as will 300,000 screens across this growing portfolio.

The acquisitions and new products were necessary to generate new revenue. Wall Street likes that as it does the positive impact the U.S. dollar's strength has had on SAP's results this year. The acquisition spree has, however, made the SAP development/integration job exponentially more difficult. The number of databases it has to support has grown with HANA and Sybase (acquired in 2010). The number of configurations has grown with on-premise, private, public and hybrid cloud varieties.

The ecosystem was already unruly, as discussed in *SAP Nation*:

> "SAP has a tendency to write code, and then hand it over to its partners. It fails to think enough about customer deployment issues. Worse, it lets customers fend for themselves in dealing with its partners. Many SAP customers have not done well negotiating with or monitoring hardware vendors, hosting firms, telco carriers, offshore application management vendors, etc. In fact, it has been suggested that unlike Ford, for SAP, "Partners are Job #1." Partner interests, it would appear, trump those of its customers. The sum total of partners' inefficiencies explains much of the excess in the SAP economy."

The ecosystem now continues to expand with Fiori, HANA specialists, HANA start-ups and private cloud providers, even as traditional systems integrators and application management providers show little in the way of "economies of repetition" even after decades and experience of thousands of projects.

Its customers in turn, have become tired of waiting and paying too much to SAP and its partners. So they are making the job for SAP even more difficult by heavily customizing, ring fencing, seeking independent support and using the many other strategies we discussed in Chapter 6.

SAP's optimistic take is that all will be fixed by the new code. I was particularly struck by one section of the Plattner/Leukert book with the tone of "change is good—don't fight it":

> "And how did our lives change with cellular phones? People do not remember anymore the lines in front of a telephone booth at the airport, or on a busy street. So, the changes will happen, and they are part of the innovation process. To fight the changes is counterproductive, it costs extra energy and may, most likely, not even work."

Taking their mobile phone analogy, the reality is that few people like their telcos, even though we love our mobile phones because the hardware, apps and games have made them so indispensable. Similarly, few customers love their ERP systems. Sure, with HANA, people will appreciate the much quicker reporting times, but the costs of the ecosystem and the project failure rates have made ERP even less attractive to many customers.

Mobile phone rates have shown steady price/performance improvements over the last few years. Such improvements have been elusive in the SAP economy and, as we saw in Chapter 5, look even less likely with S/4.

Today, enterprise customers also have many conflicting technology investment choices that they did not have a decade ago, or even five years ago. Every dollar spent on back office and IT infrastructure takes away from investments needed in digital products, services and business models.

Given all this, SAP needs to revisit its "circle." That will mean changing the scope of S/4, rethinking the ecosystem and investing in more automation to help customer migrations and operations. Another area where SAP could make its "problem bigger" is in creating customer urgency. It has been pitching the time/speed dimension around HANA and should also apply that logic to S/4 adoption. The early results suggest S/4 adoption may follow a trajectory similar to the slow pace of NetWeaver, BYD and HANA adoption in the last decade.

Hopefully, as Joy says expanding their "circle" will allow them to better understand all the moving parts in the SAP economy.

The SAP Customer "Circle"

Bruce J. Rogow is the closest thing to a Yoda that the IT Industry has today. With his background at Nolan, Norton & Co., then Gartner and now as a principal at IT Odyssey (where he criss-crosses the country visiting CIOs and cataloging their successes and challenges) and ICEX (which facilitates knowledge-exchange programs for enterprise architects and data center executives from large, mainly global firms), he has seen just about everything in our industry.

In several conversations with him as he reviewed *SAP Nation*, I have gleaned some of his concerns about the state of IT and SAP customers in particular:

- IT has always been an asset management game; however, the players today don't seem to know the game, hire the right players (enterprise architects, technology-savvy financial staff), acquire the right tools or even develop the right game plan.

- The focus of IT is now expanding to include "demand chains," the front office and revenue generation and business development as well as the Internet of Things (IoT). Over the next decade we are likely to see platforms emerge for the generation of revenue or the demand chain, much as we have seen the evolution of ERP for supply chain and back-office administration.

- There used to be real, objective, independent management consultancies that saw an ethical barrier between evaluation/risk management/making recommendations and being (what Rogow calls) the "doacy." Unlike management consultancies, doacies are firms whose primary revenue driver is the large project work of design, implementation or ongoing operations. These doacies masquerade as management consultancies, but they would benefit far more from a gigantic implementation project than from an objective analysis of client needs and capabilities. If the companies who hire doacies to do the evaluations are naïve enough to not realize the conflict of interest, they deserve the problems they encounter.

Broadly, Rogow is pointing out that we do not have many independent thinkers in IT, especially considering how complex IT has become. The challenge is particularly acute in the SAP Universe with its fragmentation and sprawl. Many consulting and customer staff have spent their entire careers on SAP projects—in particular, on older SAP products. They go to the same SAP events year after year and repeat what SAP shows them.

It's what psychologists call the "Stockholm Syndrome," where hostages develop positive feelings toward their captors and even defend and justify their actions.

As with SAP, its customers need to broaden their own problem definition. Here are some tactics for them to consider:

Rethink your talent mix

If you have never worked with a SaaS product, how can you accept that upgrades should be exponentially easier than what you have experienced? And that application management should not take armies of support staff? If you have not been involved with cutting-edge design teams, how can you question if Fiori is state-of-the-art? If you are not tasked with competitive intelligence, how can you judge which innovations are becoming commonplace in your industry and demand that from SAP? Or question consultants who glibly say SAP features constitute the "best practice"?

Many SAP customers would benefit from diversifying their staffing.

An example of that diversification comes from Dave Smoley, CIO at AstraZeneca, the large pharmaceuticals company. In *SAP Nation*, he described how he is transforming his talent base. He hired executives like Shobie Ramakrishnan, who had previously implemented several cloud applications, including a large Google Apps deployment at Genentech, the pioneering genomics company (and now a Roche subsidiary). She also ran portions of technology operations at Salesforce.

More ambitiously, Smoley is also looking to invert the 70 percent outsourced model in his SAP, infrastructure operations, application development and maintenance, cloud computing and mobile IT areas. He expects to bring over 4,000 outsourced jobs back in-house over the next three years through a network in Chennai, Silicon Valley and Eastern Europe.

You also need a realistic perspective from your staff about back-office investments and the role of SAP. Jeff Robertson, CIO of DigitalGlobe, a leading provider of earth imagery solutions, was quoted in the book as saying, "We have the best product in the market. Now we have to also make our interface with our customers the easiest." He described how his team, while evaluating Fiori, looked much more broadly at customer experience and product hierarchies. His pragmatic view on innovation: "As a leading-edge, high-tech company, our definition of innovation is in next-gen satellites and information products, not a large back-office re-implementation."

Expect more from your sourcing/vendor management groups

With churn in the SAP ecosystem, customers have to learn more about firms with skills around Fiori, HANA and new SAP acquisitions. The procurement and legal staff have to revisit hosting providers with newer cloud delivery mind-sets and rethink application support firms with more as-a-service models and automation investments. For implementations, they have to expect different delivery models. And they have to become more analytical in their monitoring of SAP and its partners, pushing for better monetary value and for continuous improvements.

Narinder Singh, co-founder of Appirio, a cloud integrator, described in *SAP Nation* the changing world of integration:

"We are really excited about the exponential combination of clouds and crowds. We believe the next step is to break down more and more of the consulting services world to be delivered as-a-service, like a utility. We believe crowdsourcing is incredibly powerful, but design/development/data science are only one part of delivering a successful result for a client. Over time, the entire consulting lifecycle will be more and more repeatable, allowing services to be knit together like software components/services and scaled up and down like cloud technology is today."

The book also described how CIO David Cooper tackled Project Slingshot at British Gas, a complex project comprising a CRM system, a billing system, a digital online solution, a data warehouse and a complete migration of all the customer data. In turn, this has enabled smart meter reading, customer engagement and analytics for customer service agents. The systems integration arrangement was one many sourcing staff should emulate:

"The systems integration contract was outcome-based with a number of protection mechanisms in place. Cooper says the key was choosing an implementation partner like Cognizant with an appropriate cultural fit and with appropriate governance and senior relationships established between the two companies. Cognizant's fees and payments were tied to specific milestones such as the number of customers migrated. The 18-month implementation has progressed fairly smoothly even though at peak the project had over 350 resources. Nearly 40 percent of the effort exerted in the project focused on testing tasks to prevent the type of problems and the poor press seen in the previous B2C project."

CLP Group, one of SAP's largest utility customers, shared detailed metrics it uses to measure SAP as well as other operational suppliers. Its SAS systems scores are a composite of various safety, quality, cost, delivery and support attributes. These scores are meant to give a supplier a 360-degree view on how it is performing. The program also gives the supplier, in return, an opportunity to score CLP.

Andre Blumberg, CLP's IT Director, described what the utility shared with SAP in a SAS review meeting:

> "We discussed joint projects—like the recent successful rollout of the SAP Business Planning and Consolidation across all of CLP's regional group companies. But, we also gave very specific feedback. We pointed out several high-severity tickets were open for over 150 days and the most serious one for 275 days. Part of it relates to how SAP sales and support is organized on a global basis. Even more telling, CLP also shared with the SAP executives the many IT initiatives it had missed out on in the previous couple of years."

The scorecard CLP uses could be adapted by other customers to help with a more fact-based relationship with SAP.

Push for more customer advocacy

When I wrote *SAP Nation*, I was struck by the lack of oversight in the SAP economy. Customers need to push for more advocacy on their behalf, especially as the S/4 rollout could potentially lead to even more inflation.

Here are a few market-watchers customers should expect more from:

User Groups
I had interviewed executives at ASUG and DSAG, the user groups representing North American and German-speaking SAP customers, respectively. They are the two largest in a global network of such groups. DSAG has been particularly forceful in challenging SAP every time it has tried to charge customers more for software maintenance. But that only accounted for roughly $10 billion out of $204 billion a year in our SAP economy model. Neither user group has focused much on all the additional "surround costs" in the SAP economy. Customers should rightly expect more advocacy from the 30 such regional user groups around the world.

Market Analysts
Firms like Forrester, Gartner and IDC often have 10–40 analysts who cover different aspects of a large technology vendor like SAP, but they do not often employ integrative models. I had to reach out to several analysts to help validate small segments of my model of the SAP economy. Other market analysts were more defensive. One questioned why I was even modeling the SAP economy when I am "not a full-time analyst." Another declined, saying it is a "sensitive topic." Customers should expect analysts to take more of the customer perspective as they cover SAP and the ERP marketplace and to better weave the research across their silos.

Technology Media

I interviewed Chris Kanaracus, previously of the IDG News Service, who had broken several stories of failed SAP projects over the last few years. He told me he rigorously mined court and SEC filings for his stories. Surprisingly, few other journalists mined similar sources, and Kanaracus has since moved on to work on ASUG where he is not expected to report on such failures. German media is very interested in SAP given its headquarters there, but tends to focus more on its executives, its financial results and the globalization challenges at SAP rather than its customers or failed projects. Again, customers have a right for technology media to look at SAP from their lens.

Academia

With SAP's annual economy in the range of the GDP of countries like Ireland, and with investments in SAP one of largest categories of capex for over a decade in the Western world, I had expected to find plenty of academic research around such investments, but that is not the case. The limited amount of research tended to focus on the impact of an announcement of such projects on the buying company's stock performance, not after-the-fact analysis of business value from the investment.

Regulators

While the FTC monitors telcos and the SEC watches for revenue recognition issues at software companies, the technology sector is generally unregulated, so I did not expect to find much data from U.S. regulators on the SAP economy. However, the EU has gone after Microsoft, Intel and Google for anticompetitive complaints. It has even gone after European telcos around mobile roaming charges. In Berlin, Sigmar Gabriel, the German Vice Chancellor and Economics Minister, "is investigating whether Germany can classify Google as a vital part of the country's infrastructure, and thus make it subject to heavy state regulation."[97] None of those vendors have had the financial impact that SAP has had on corporate customers. European regulators have, however, stayed away from SAP, even with its dominant—estimated at 50 percent—ERP market share in German-speaking Europe.

During the recent financial crisis around Greece, the *Washington Post* wrote, "The euro is a unique experiment in monetary governance without a government."[98]

The SAP economy similarly has no government. Many customer executives will say they have little time or interest to "influence the influencers" discussed above. You cannot blame them, but then they need to increase their own oversight to help protect their interests.

✳ ✳ ✳

At the beginning of the book, we asked several questions like:

> Will SAP Nation have a smooth transition with its recently announced S/4 or will it be chaotic, with people sighing in relief as they exit its airspace?

and

> Will McDermott's "underdogs" deliver a stunning turnaround?

---

[97] http://www.nytimes.com/2014/10/11/opinion/sunday/why-germans-are-afraid-of-google.html?_r=0

[98] http://www.washingtonpost.com/rweb/politics/why-the-euro-is-in-trouble/2015/06/28/3446f35a0cb3c28a0e60b3455147aabf_story.html?tid=kindle-app

This book provided some perspectives on how those and other questions may be answered. Much better answers will come over the next few years as a result of the circle that SAP re-draws around S/4 and the thousands of circles its customers are drawing.

There's nothing wrong in re-thinking and re-launching a product. Brian Chesky, co-founder of the wildly successful hospitality exchange Airbnb, recently tweeted:

> "If you launch and no one notices, launch again. We launched 3 times."

I look forward to cataloging the S/4 evolution and other SAP and customer driven shifts in the economy in SAP Nation 3.0.

Index

↝